When I talk with people who listen to "Hour of Power" week after week, they often ask me: "Where does your father find all of his stories?" I tell them he finds his stories the same way Jesus Christ found His, in everyday situations. Everyone who is active and alive today has a story to tell. My father has the ability to see the positive, the uplifting, and the inspiring side in every situation. . . . This is what he calls "possibility thinking." This is what produces positive attitudes. This is what moves mountains and changes lives . . .

—Robert A. Schuller

ROBERT SCHULLER'S

LIFE CHANGERS

Edited by his son
ROBERT A. SCHULLER

A JOVE BOOK

Note to reader: Complete indexes of titles,
topics, and names begin on page 171.

This Jove book contains the complete
text of the original hardcover edition.
It has been completely reset in a typeface
designed for easy reading, and was printed
from new film.

ROBERT SCHULLER'S LIFE CHANGERS

A Jove Book / published by arrangement with
Fleming H. Revell Company

PRINTING HISTORY
Fleming H. Revell edition published 1981
Jove edition / June 1983
Second printing / June 1984

ISBN: C-515-08163-9

Introduction

It has been said that the secret of a great speaker is the ability to tell a good story. When I talk with people who listen to "Hour of Power" week after week, they often ask me: "Where does your father find all of his stories? They're so good!" I tell them that he finds his stories the same way Jesus Christ found His, in everyday situations. Everyone who is active and alive today has a story to tell. Depending upon the way it is told, it can become positive or negative, uplifting or deflating, inspiring or demeaning. My father has the ability to see the positive, the uplifting, and the inspiring side in every situation and story. This is because he understands the reality behind the promise of Romans 8:28: "All things work together for good to those who love God." He understands that God can turn "Scars Into Stars"; that a greater good can develop from tragedy, if we only believe and have faith in our benevolent and omnipotent

God. This is what he calls "possibility thinking." This is what produces positive attitudes. This is what moves mountains and changes lives. With this attitude you will see the positive, the uplifting, and the inspiring side of every situation and story in your life.

This book is a compilation of my father's best stories. Some are funny, some are inspiring, others enlightening, and all of them are positive. It has many functions:

1. This book can be read simply for the enjoyment, the inspiration, and the enlightenment that its pages contain.
2. It can be read as a devotional. Simply read one story every morning, and you'll receive a little positive boost.
3. This book can be used as a spiritual pharmacy. In the back of the book is an index which can be your guide to finding the exact story you need to lift you out of a negative attitude.
4. This book can be used as a resource for speakers. As one prepares his message he can use the index to find the story he needs to illustrate his point.

No matter what your reason is for reading this book I'm sure that you will find it positive, uplifting, inspiring, enlightening and humorous.

ROBERT SCHULLER'S LIFE CHANGERS

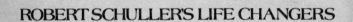

Carol's Arabian Colt

Some of you may know that my daughter Carol was nearly killed in a motorcycle accident and did have to have her left leg amputated. Carol loves to ride horses, and as a gift, she was sent a magnificently beautiful, purebred Arabian colt by Doug Griffith of Imperial Farms in Baltimore, Maryland. The sire of this colt is a purebred Egyptian; the dam, or mother, is pure domestic Arabian. This beautiful animal has a fantastically impressive bloodline. When the cargo plane landed in the Los Angeles airport, and the elevator lowered this noble creature to the ground, his royal lineage showed itself in the way he arched his neck and tail, flared his nostrils, and tipped his elegant head. There is tremendous potential for greatness in this young colt, but he needs training.

Carol has been training this horse to lunge. Carol is a great inspiration to me, for when she trains the

colt, she stands on her one good leg and uses a crutch
in place of her other leg. With her free hand, she
holds the lead rope and her other crutch. Already the
colt is responding beautifully to her training. At her
command, he walks slowly, then trots in a circle
around Carol, as she balances on her one leg and piv-
ots to face him. The horse knows her touch and
readily obeys her command. It's a remarkable, inspiring sight to see this beautiful growing relationship
between a fourteen-year-old girl and an animal of
princely bloodlines.

Yesterday, while I was meditating and praying in
my bedroom on the other side of the house, Carol
was lunging the horse with her schoolmate. (We
won't allow her to train alone, until she has her prosthesis and can use both legs again.) In a rare moment,
the horse raised its head sharply, caught Carol a little
off balance, and pulled the rope out of her hands. As
the rope fell, it hit the horse's hoof and spooked him.
He took off and ran around some trees, but as he
ran, the rope only became more entangled about his
front hoof, which really frightened him. So like his
ancestors who ran against the wind through the great
desert sand dunes of Cairo and carried their masters
to safety in battle, the colt flew across the lawn. And
as a bird fails to see the clear glass of a window, so
the horse did not see the glass of our sliding doors
and exploded through them into our living room.

I've never seen a bull in a china closet, but I've
seen a gelding in a living room! I was meditating
when I heard the most thunderous explosion of shat-
tering glass that I've ever heard in my life. I leaped
out of bed and ran into the hallway to see the rear
end of the horse, Hofstar, disappear into the kitchen

as he sauntered into Carol's bedroom! You can't imagine what it's like, living in the Schuller household —never a dull moment!

My brother, who came for my oldest daughter's wedding and stayed to enjoy the peace and quiet, cornered the Arabian colt in the closet. Fortunately the horse was not injured, though he did appear to be quite embarrassed. But the living-room floor was showered with glass.

When my wife arrived home from her Saturday-morning shopping, our twelve-year-old daughter, Gretchen, ran to greet her with the latest news. "Mom," she cried, "you'll never guess what happened!" "What happened?" my wife asked. "Wait 'til you see what the horse did in the house!" She exclaimed. "It's a mess!"

Well, that's life at our place. But you know, Carol went right back to training Hofstar. She really loves that horse; we all do. We recognize that his great ancestry gives him tremendous potential, just as God loves you and sees your tremendous potential. You can't imagine the extent of the potential and intelligence you have inherited from your ancestors. You are a descendant from God! Like you, your ancestors were made in His image. All you need is God's training and control. That's why Jesus Christ wants to be your Savior. He wants to bring out the potential that lies within you and transform you so that others can find strength and comfort in you.

Try Giving Yourself Away

Years ago I read a story in a book entitled *Try Giving Yourself Away* by David Dunn. The author told about a woman in the lobby of the Union Depot in Cincinnati, Ohio, waiting for the train. She saw a young girl, about fifteen years of age, sitting alone in the corner of the depot. Then she saw a mother with two crying children and an armload of packages enter the train station and sit down across from the young girl. Before the woman could get settled into her seat, the teenage girl hopped up and ran over to her. "Can I take care of your two children while you go out to get something to eat?" she asked. "You look a little tired and the next train isn't due for a while, so why don't you let me help you? I'm very good with children." Startled, the mother said, "Oh, thank you! That would be wonderful." And she left the two little girls in the care of this anonymous and generous babysitter.

A little later the mother returned looking relaxed and refreshed. "Thank you so much," she said. And the young girl enthused, "Are you catching the next train?" "Yes," she replied, "as soon as I can get everything together." "Let me help you," the young helper said. And then she gathered all of the lady's packages and headed towards the train. After they boarded, she waved and said good-bye. Then she turned and went back into the train lobby and sat down.

She wasn't seated more than ten minutes when she spotted another mother with children. So she walked over and volunteered to baby-sit once again. And after a while that mother boarded the train, and then this drifting helper found another mother and did the same thing.

By this time the observer was puzzled, so she approached the young girl and said, "I'm curious. I've been watching you for an hour or so, and you've spent the entire time helping these young mothers and their children. Why are you doing this?"

"Oh," she said, "I was one of five children. My dad was in the army and we were always moving from once place to another. My mom got so tired carrying the packages and suitcases and caring for all of us. I remember her saying to me, 'You are so good with children.'

"My dad went to war in Europe and he never came back, so that left my mom alone. And she just recently died, so I thought that maybe I could do something for others because she said I was so good with kids. I thought there would be a lot of mothers who would be tired here so that's why I come to the depot! It makes me feel good. It really helps."

That's understanding Christianity the self-sacrificial way—and it's wonderful!

Let It Flow

Frank Laubach, one of the great inspiring persons in my life, tells a story about the time he was in India and decided to take a tour of a new electro-generating plant. He saw an enormous dam, which was used for the production of electrical energy. He took an elevator down to see the massive turbines driven by the pressure of water against the curved vanes of the wheels. But he noticed that no electricity was being generated. "Why isn't energy being produced?" he asked the tour guide. "I mean, there's the dam, the water, and the turbines; why isn't it working?" And the guide replied, "The valve is closed. The water is not flowing through right now. And until the valve is open and the water flows through, there is no power produced."

If you come to church and absorb the message, but keep it within yourself and don't share it with your friends at the office throughout the week, or with your wife and your children, it doesn't flow through. You don't understand it. Christianity is Christ being accepted into my heart; into my mind; into my life; and then flowing through me—out of me, reaching the people who need my love.

Gail Bartosh

I want to share with you about a person named Gail Bartosh. She and her parents have been members of this church almost from the very beginning. In the early days of our ministry, when we had only a couple hundred members, her father, Francis, was an elder of the church. Our communion set was dedicated to him when he passed away. I remember Francis used to say to me, "I wonder what will happen to Gail." Although no one ever said much about it, some thought Gail was mongoloid; others thought she was mentally retarded.

Today, Gail is one of the greatest workers we have

in this church. She works in the nursery and cares for more than two hundred infants a week. During the week, Gail works in our day-care center. She beautifully and lovingly cares for these little children of all nationalities, creeds, and colors while their working mothers make a living for their families. Gail is a terrific girl, and God is using her to touch so many young lives.

Recently Gail went into the hospital for a checkup and a lump was discovered in her breast. She went into surgery for removal of the lump, but the doctors decided that her condition required a radical mastectomy. So at age thirty-seven, Gail lost her breast. I went to call on her the other day, and found her weeping into the pillows. She said, "Doctor Schuller, look at me. Now Mother has a mentally retarded cancer victim on her hands." I reached over and took her hand and said, "No, Gail, you're wrong! Wrong! *Wrong!* Your mother has a bright, brave, beautiful, inspiring gal on her hands. Now you say that." And smiling through the tears, she repeated with perfect diction, "Now Mother has a bright, brave, beautiful, inspiring gal on her hands."

"You know, Doctor Schuller," she continued, "when I was a child I was taken from one doctor to another and none could agree exactly what was wrong with me. One doctor would say, 'She's a mongoloid.' Another doctor would say, 'No, she's not a mongoloid; she's mentally retarded.' And still another would insist, 'She isn't mentally retarded; she's just slow.' So finally I stopped seeing doctors, started going to church, and decided to develop the potential God has given me the very best I could."

And that is exactly what Gail Bartosh has done.

She touches the lives of children daily and inspires them to be beautiful, brave, and successful persons. She decided to make the most of what she had, and she has become a fantastic human being.

Whether you realize it or not, you have the inherited potential for greatness. All you have to do is let God hold the lead line, and He will train and control you. You will be pleasantly surprised when you see the life that can be yours, as you put yourself in the Master's hands.

Mom Schug's Love

I conducted the funeral service for a woman that I called Mom Schug. Her real name was Bernice Schug, and she thought of me as her adopted son. She was well into her eighties when she passed away, peacefully and swiftly like a flower that had come to full bloom and was ready to drop its petals, so the new seeds could sprout. She lived the full cycle! I saw Mom Schug hours before she passed away in the hospital. We talked and prayed together. She smiled and her dimples were as bright as when she was a girl. Her eyes were as attractive and saucy as when she was sixteen. Only a week before her death, she had been working at our twenty-four-hour New Hope Telephone Counseling service.

Mom was a poor woman. She lived in a tiny mobile home that she bought thirty years ago. But every Sunday she would take 10 percent of her Social Security check and place it into the offering plate at our church.

Dear Mom Schug, what a happy woman! Oh, you may say, "She had a good life. She had such few problems." The truth is, she lost her only son, Bob, years ago in World War II. He enlisted in the navy, so he could join the fight to liberate our country from a horrible war. Bob was in the Pacific when he was struck by a shell in his leg. They quickly transported him down to the medics. Doctors were preparing to amputate his leg when a Kamikaze pilot, on a suicide dive, struck the side of the ship right where the medical center was, killing Bob, the medical team, and many others. What a crushing grief that was to Bernice Schug. But you know, God can take a crushing grief, and He can come rushing in! Mom Schug found a joy in her sorrow because she experienced the perfect love that came from God.

Several years later, Mom received the bulletin from our church and saw that a former Japanese Kamikaze pilot was going to be the guest on the following Sunday. She couldn't believe it! Days before he was to carry out his suicide plunge, the war ended. He went back to Japan and there he met a missionary and was introduced to Jesus Christ. Now, he was traveling around the world, sharing his testimony of what Jesus Christ had done in his life. Mom Schug called me and said, "Bob, I don't think I'll be in church this Sunday," and told me why. "Well, Mom," I replied, "I can understand. You are human. If you don't want to come to church, then stay home and pray or read your Bible, or watch a church service on TV."

Saturday came and I received another call. "Bob," Mom Schug exclaimed, "are you sure you are going through with this?" "Yes," I answered, "this man is a terrific Christian. He has a personal relationship with Jesus Christ.'' She said good-bye, and I could hear her sobbing on the other end of the line. The next morning, the church was filling up fast, when I saw her come in through the side door and sit in the back row. She figured that she could sneak out before the service was over.

The service began with a few hymns and then the guest approached the podium. He shared a beautiful testimony and then closed with prayer. This was the time when Mom was supposed to have slipped out, but she forgot. By the time she opened her eyes to still try to make an early exit, the Japanese man was standing only a few feet away from her. She could have exited out the side door or gone down the aisle, but she didn't. Instead she walked over to the man, opened her arms, and embraced him. She whispered in his ear about her son and tears started streaming down both of their faces. When you've got love in your heart and Jesus Christ in your life, you can love the unlovely.

True Confession

A priest, a rabbi, and a Protestant minister got together and decided to talk openly about themselves. The first religious leader was very frank, admitting some sins that he had committed. The other two men were shocked. Their mouths fell open, and they became quite flushed. The rabbi was next, so he regained his composure and walked to the front of the room. He began, ''Normally I could never confess this, but since my friend was open and honest I will be, too!" And he confessed every sin that he had committed. Then came the Protestant's turn, so he stood before the group and said, "Well, I would never have dared confess my secret sin, but after hearing my colleagues openly admit their sins, I will, too. I admit that I'm an incurable gossip. I can't keep a secret and I can hardly wait to get out of here!"

"Mount Everest, You Can't Get Any Bigger!"

When I was in London, England, a couple of weeks ago, I visited a hall where a man named Mallory was honored with a banquet years ago. In the 1920s Mallory led an expedition to try to conquer Mount Everest. The first expedition failed, as did the second. Then, with a team of the best quality and ability, Mallory made a third assault. But in spite of careful planning and extensive safety precautions, disaster struck: an avalanche hit, and Mallory and most of his party were killed.

When the few who did survive returned to England, they held a glorious banquet saluting the great people of Mallory's final expedition. As the leader of the survivors stood to acknowledge the applause, he looked around the hall at the framed pictures of Mallory and his comrades who had died. Then he turned his back to the crowds to face the huge picture of Mount Everest, which stood looming like a silent, unconquerable giant behind the banquet table.

With tears streaming down his face, he addressed the mountain on behalf of Mallory and his dead friends. "I speak to you, Mount Everest, in the name of all brave men living and those yet unborn," he began. "Mount Everest, you defeated us once; you defeated us twice; you defeated us three times. But Mount Everest, we shall someday defeat you, because you can't get any bigger and we can!"

Where are you today? Whether you find yourself at home, in a lonely hotel room, a hospital, or a prison, possibility thinking can work for you to perform healing of body, mind and soul. It will help you to see that Jesus Christ wants to come into your life and transform you. When you give your life to Jesus, you will become a beautiful new creature. Doors will open. Freedom will come your way. And when you run into problems, you will have the calm assurance that they can't get any bigger—but you can!

Never Listen to a Negative Thought

Negative ideas multiply rapidly. If you want to attract tuna, you use one kind of bait; if you use a different kind of bait, you'll attract the sharks. A negative idea manifested in a moment of self-pity, jealousy, resentment, or anger—even a simple, seemingly innocent moment of unkind thought—harbored, nurtured, and acted upon, can be very destructive in its ultimate consequence.

Once there was a devoted pastor who counseled a

woman suffering from a very rare, fatal disease. A secretary in the church saw them together and started a rumor that he was being unfaithful to his wife. The pastor could not defend himself without violating a pastoral confidence. When the woman died, the true story came out. The church board and the intimates knew that there was no foundation to that ill-fated rumor at all. But nevertheless, his reputation had been demolished in the community. When the pastor discovered the source of the rumor, he called the secretary, who was quick to come. In tears, she lamented, "I don't know how to apologize. What can I ever do to set things right again?" "Here's what I want you to do," he replied. He gave her a pillow full of goose feathers and said, "Go to the high hill outside of town. When the wind blows, just let the feathers fly, and bring back the empty pillow." "Oh, thank you," she cried. She went to the hill and scattered the feathers to the wind. When she returned, she showed the pastor the empty pillow and asked, "Now, can things be as they were? Will you forgive me?" "One last thing," the pastor said, "go back and pick up all the feathers."

If you respond to a negative thought, it will come back to you.

Cast Your Bread on the Waters

Cast your bread on the waters and it will come back to you!

Ecclesiastes 11:1

When I first began studying this verse, I came to the conclusion that it honestly didn't make much sense. If you throw seeds on the water, they will float back to the shore, *if* the current flows in the right direction. But if you throw bread on the water, it will dissolve; it will get soggy. And if it does come back, I don't think any of us would care to eat it. The text doesn't make much sense, until you realize that the phrase was originally spoken in a culture where fish provided the basis for economic survival. If you throw bread on the water, the bread itself will not be edible, but it will attract the fish to the surface so you can net them.

Years ago, Mrs. Schuller and I bought a two-acre parcel of ground in the country. The previous owner had made several little fish ponds, so I put water in the ponds and bought a bunch of two-inch-long, little koi fish. Since that time, they have done very well and have multiplied to number more than two hundred. Koi fish are beautiful Japanese carp and come in more than forty-seven colors and varieties. They are unusually tame; they will eat out of my hand. I can caress them on the back, and they really like it. If I don't see them lurking behind the lily pads, all I have to do is throw a piece of bread down, and they surface from out of the deep to congregate near the surface of the water. That's what the writer of Ecclesiastes had in mind. If you're hungry, take your bread and throw it into the water. You'll lose your bread, but you'll come back with a meal for the whole family!

Like a crust of bread, a God-given idea can attract enormous resources that come from far corners, out of the darkness. Hold this Bible verse in your mind today: "Cast your bread on the waters and it will return to you." When you give to God, your gift will really return to you multiplied.

There Is a Purpose to Everything

Not long ago, I sat next to a man on a plane and he asked me what I did. I told him I was a minister. "What do you do?" I asked. "I'm a gambler," he replied, tossing a silver dollar carelessly into the air. "Do you have a faith?" I inquired. "Yes," he replied, "I believe there is a purpose to everything on planet earth." "That sounds like good theology," I responded. "I really believe that," he asserted. Then, as if he were testing me, he challenged, "What's the purpose of a mouse?" Frankly, he caught me speechless. I hadn't the foggiest idea what the purpose of a mouse could be. But he had an answer on the tip of his tongue. "The purpose of a mouse," he explained, "is to generate job opportunities." "How can a mouse generate job opportunities?" I asked. Then he told me exactly how many jobs in our economy exist to deal with the problem of mice. He rattled off the number of people that work in factories that make mouse traps and produce mouse-control poisons. And he cited the billions of dollars spent each year on cat food. As he went on and on, I was impressed. I thanked God for these lousy mice! And I've been grateful for them ever since.

Ecology has taught us there is a purpose to everything under the sun. The delicate balance between every earthly element ties the whole dynamic creation together. And if there's a purpose to the wind, the water, the plants, insects, and even mice, then you can be sure there's a purpose for human beings. It is good psychology, good theology, and good biblical interpretation to say that our purpose on planet earth is to develop our God-given creative potential that we might truly glorify our heavenly Father. When we do that, we make God's creation more beautiful, and we leave the world a better place because we lived in it.

Look in Unlikely Places

A couple of years ago, I was invited to go up to Vancouver, Canada, to lecture to about two hundred ministers representative of the religious groups of that great province. At the opening of the conference, I recall meeting the treasurer. He was seated at the registration desk where he collected money to cover the expenses of food, lodging, and rental of the auditorium for the conference. When all the members had registered, he had a total of about six thousand dollars in cash, which he put in a little metal box. When the conference opened, he began to feel very nervous about carrying that much cash, so he put the money in the safest place he could think of— in the trunk of his car. That afternoon, after the last lecture, he went to the garage to get his car and found it was gone. It had been stolen! Downcast, he reported the theft to the police.

Five or six days later, the police found the car abandoned. It had been completely stripped. An officer called the man and informed him that they had found his car. To add insult to injury, he had to pay to have the car towed back home. But amazingly, when he opened the trunk, there was the little metal box still holding the entire six thousand dollars! The thief had never bothered to look for anything of value in the trunk.

The truth is that we oftentimes overlook the greatest potential and value, because we simply can't envision such a productive concept coming from such an unlikely source. Some of the greatest concepts come out of the most unlikely ideas. When God comes into your mind, He will give you ideas that will enable you to develop your possibilities to their fullest potential.

Your Problem Is Not a Banyan Tree

On my first trip to Thailand, I went on an elephant hunt in the jungle. The wild elephants come thundering out of the jungle into an arena, and a massive log gate is dropped to close off the exit. Once the elephant is made captive, the men tie the end of a long chain around the elephant's foot. The other end is tied to a huge banyan tree. The great elephant will pull with all its strength, but it can't budge the banyan tree. Finally, after struggling for days and weeks the elephant will barely lift its ponderous foot, and when it feels the chain just begin to become taut, it drops its foot heavily to the ground, because it knows further struggle is useless. The elephant surrenders to the chain.

At this point, the hunters know the elephant is really trapped forever. For when they take the elephant and chain it to a little iron stake by a circus tent, the elephant never attempts to pull away, because it still thinks it is chained to a banyan tree. The elephant never realizes how easily it could achieve freedom.

God's love tells you that you are not chained to a banyan tree! Your problem is not insurmountable! Perhaps you're in the hospital, and you are fighting disease. Remember, disease is not a banyan tree. Maybe you're having problems in marriage. Remember, your problem is not a banyan tree; it is a stake.

Love Liberates

One of my most delightful memories as a small child on our Iowa farm is of the days in the spring when we would receive our little baby chicks. I used to take the soft, fuzzy, newly hatched little things and rub what felt like silky fur against my cheek. Sometimes I would squeeze too tightly, because I loved them so much, and I didn't want them to get away. "Don't hold so tight," my father warned. "But I love it so," I protested. "If you love it so much," he said, "you have to let go."

If you really love your wife, don't be so possessive;

if you love your husband, don't be so jealous. Real
love is not possessive; it does not manipulate or in-
timidate. Real love liberates. God's love is like that.
First He elevates you beyond the guilt that could give
you a negative self-image, which would cause you to
lose all self-confidence and render you woefully and
totally ineffective. Then He sets you free to become
the person you were meant to be.

Sheila's Dream

Many years ago my daughter Sheila was at a very low
point emotionally. Ever since she was in the fifth
grade she wanted to be a medical doctor and serve as
a missionary. Finally she graduated from Hope
College with a major in chemistry and a grade point
average somewhere between an *A* and a *B*. But there
were fifty-four thousand graduating seniors applying
for medical school and only fourteen thousand
openings in all the medical schools in the United
States. She was one of the forty thousand not accepted. Now she had to decide whether she would
study for her master's degree, and then reapply for
medical school, or make a mid-flight correction. She
chose the latter, because she discovered the real
reason she wanted to be a doctor was because she
wanted to be a part of a ministry of healing. She concluded she didn't have to be an M.D. to do that. So
she tried to find herself through ministry in the youth
department of our church.
    Somewhere along the line she had an unfortunate,
heartbreaking experience with a young man. They

simply were not meant for each other, and the relationship left her with a deeply negative self-image. One morning she and I were sitting around the table in the kitchen and I quietly asked, "Sheila, what do you really want out of life?" With tears streaming down her face, she poured out her heart. "Dad, I guess all I really want is a home like the one I was raised in. I want children like my brother and sisters."

She paused for a moment, and as I gently brushed the tears from her cheeks, I cried too. "You know," she continued, "I don't care if I have a husband who's rich or famous. I don't have to have a man like that. All I want is a man who will treat me like a precious gem."

As we wept together, I shared her inner anguish and lovingly assured her, "Sheila, that is a noble dream. God will give you someone like that." All persons—whether they are little or grown, young and strong, or bent-backed and old—need somebody who will treat them like precious gems. That's why we, as clergy, still challenge the groom and the bride to take each other for better or worse. Those vows signify a commitment to care forever. Every person needs someone who will treat him or her like a precious gem! God does that for us.

Casting all your care upon Him for He cares for you.

1 Peter 5:7

Never Count Up the Might-Have-Beens

I was born and raised on an Iowa farm. I vividly remember the dust-bowl years. When I was a child, in the thirties, the drought swept in from the Dakotas. The wind was dry; the wind was dusty; the wind was violent; and the wind was fierce. The wind became our enemy, because it would peel the dry, rich, black soil, and swirl it like drifting dunes in the gullies and canyons of our fields. We prayed for the rains, but the rains did not come. I shall never forget that difficult year. We walked around our farm with white towels over our faces to keep from suffocating in the driving dust.

Then harvest season came. My father would normally harvest a hundred wagons full of corn. But I remember the harvest that year. My father harvested not the one hundred wagon loads we usually harvested—but a meager one-half wagon load. I can see the old wagon standing in the yard—only half-full. It was a total crop disaster that has never been equalled before or since!

You know what happened? I shall never forget it. Seated at the dinner table with his calloused hands holding ours, my father looked up and thanked God. He said, "I thank You, God, that I have lost nothing. I have regained the seed I planted in the springtime!" He used a half-wagon load for seed, he got a half-wagon load back. His attitude of gratitude was that he didn't lose a thing, while other farmers were saying, "We lost ninety loads," or, "We lost one hundred loads." They counted their losses by what they hoped they could have accomplished. And I'll never forget my father saying, "You can never count up the might-have-beens or you will be defeated." Never look at what you have lost; look at what you have left. Those words of wisdom from my father, who never went past the sixth grade, were immeasurable in making me the possibility thinker that I am today. The attitude of gratitude gave my father surviving power. He went right back and planted that seed the next year. When he finally retired, he was no longer a poor farmer. With this attitude he prepared and left a nice estate for his children.

High-Flying Balloons

A man was selling balloons on the streets of New York City. He knew how to attract a crowd before he offered his wares for sale. He took a white balloon, filled it up, and let it float upward. Next he filled a red balloon, and released it. Then he added a yellow one. As the red, yellow, and white balloons were floating above his head, the little children gathered around to buy his balloons. A hesitant black boy looked up at the balloons and finally asked, "If you filled a black balloon, would it go up too?" The man looked down and said, "Why, sure! It's not the color of the balloon, it's what's inside that makes it go up!"

What's inside of you determines whether you achieve peak success experiences in your life. Climbing to the peak depends upon your mind and your attitudes.

The Great Houdini

It's fascinating to read the stories, many of them legendary, about the late Houdini. That masterful magician was probably a better locksmith than he was a magician. He had a standing challenge that he could get out of any locked jail in sixty minutes, providing they would let him enter in his regular street clothes and not watch him work.

One of the stories is about a little town in the British Isles that decided to challenge (and perhaps embarrass) the great Houdini. This town had just completed an escape-proof jail, and so the townfolk invited Houdini to come to see if he could break out.

He accepted the challenge. He was allowed to enter the jail in his street clothes. People said they saw the locksmith turn the lock some strange way, and then with the clang of steel, everybody turned their backs and left him alone to work. Houdini had hidden a long flexible steel rod in his belt, which is what he used to try to trip the lock. He worked for thirty minutes. He kept his ear close to the lock—forty-five minutes, and then an hour passed; he was perspiring. After two hours, he was exhausted. He leaned against the door, and to his amazement, it fell open. They had never locked the door! It was their trick on the great escape artist!

The door was locked only in Houdini's mind. That's the *only* place it was locked! Some of you think that you can't overcome your problem. The only place where it is impossible is in your thinking. That's the only thing that's locked!

The Treacherous Coral Sea

Some years ago, Mrs. Schuller and I were faculty members on the Chapman College Campus Afloat. We were on the ship for the summer, sailing to the South Seas. I shall never forget the time when the captain said that the next day the ship would go through a very narrow crevice in the Coral Sea. The following day, we were told the ship was approaching the crevice. The passengers were all on deck. We were told the ship needed thirty feet of water to avoid grounding. In the shallow coral regions that we were passing through, there was only one place where the water was deeper than thirty feet, and this passageway was so narrow that I had the impression that it was hardly wide enough for our ship. To maneuver such a huge ship through such a narrow crevice was indeed precarious.

As we came closer, the captain cut the forward speed, and then off in the distance we saw a little motorboat coming toward us, leaving its wide white wake. In that motorboat was a special captain in uniform from Australia. He stepped out onto our ship through a little hole down below. You could see him come in. He came up the elevator, and the captain of our ship saluted him and stepped aside. And this special captain from Australia took the helm, because he specialized in taking ships through this narrow passage. That was teamwork.

You know who that special pilot must be for you, don't you? His name is Jesus Christ. Make sure that Jesus Christ is at the helm and, as you go through some narrow waters, you'll reach port safely.

"What's Green Bay Without the Packers?"

One day I sat next to a man on a plane in Los Angeles. "Where are you from?" he asked me. "Garden Grove, California," I enthused. And then—he insulted me. "Garden Grove? I never heard of it." "Where are you from?" I inquired, hoping it would be a town I had never heard of. "Green Bay, Wisconsin," he replied, which, unfortunately, I had heard of, being a Packer fan.

Then I thought, *How can I insult him back without violating my Christian ethics or self-respect and self-esteem?* That was challenging. I came up with what I considered to be an ethical, subtle, clever, Christian insult. "Green Bay?" I questioned, looking him straight in the eye, "What does Green Bay have outside the Packers?" "I don't have the faintest idea," he exclaimed, "I'm the coach!" "How are you going to do next season?" I asked. "Terrific!" he enthused. "Well, how can you say that?" I countered. "Because," he said, "we've got talent." "Talent? Is that right? What's talent?" I questioned.

Since he was a coach, I thought he'd say "speed" or "coordination," or maybe "intelligence"; but he didn't reply with any of those answers. "Talent? Why, it's character!" he exclaimed. "What do you mean by 'character'?" I queried. "I mean loyalty to the team, that's what I mean," he answered.

Success isn't a matter of having *things,* it's a matter of having the right thoughts, character, integrity, enthusiasm, and determination. God wants you to be a success, because God wants you to enjoy self-esteem. You are His child, not just a glorified monkey. If He gave you a thing, it wouldn't feed your self-esteem; but when He gives you an idea, it leads you to success. You gain wholesome self-respect in the process of achieving. So, you can be sure it is God who is feeding you with those success-generating ideas and opportunities.

The Ray Kroc Story

Have you ever gone by a store that had lousy management and then, one day you passed by and saw a banner that read UNDER NEW MANAGEMENT? It's amazing what can happen when management changes.

Some years ago, there were a couple of brothers named McDonald who owned a hamburger shop in San Bernardino. Then along came a fifty-nine-year-old man with a thousand dollars to invest—and a better idea about how the shop should be managed. He bought the brothers out. His name is Ray Kroc. He brought to the business fresh new ideas, and that's what made the difference. Today *McDonald's* is a world-wide, multimillion dollar enterprise.

Maybe you think you're doing a pretty good job managing your life, but you haven't seen anything—until you let your life come under the management of Jesus Christ. Fly a new banner across your mind that declares UNDER NEW MANAGEMENT. Receive Him as your Savior—as your Lord—and say, "From this time on, I'm going to talk to You; I'm going to walk with You; I'm going to love You; and I'm going to let You call the shots in my life."

The Influence of the Insignificant

Once there was a dear lady named Hazel who loved to sing simple, common gospel songs. She decided to try out for the church choir. She told the choir director that she couldn't read music, so he said, "We'll let you sing, but just stay on tune." But she couldn't stay on tune, so she had to drop out of the choir. Nothing really seemed to have any meaning in Hazel's life. Her mother had recently died. When Hazel was young, she had spent most of her time caring for her mother, instead of dating and enjoying her adolescence. Consequently, she had never married.

At the age of sixty, she felt as though she had failed in her attempt to find happiness in life. Alone, with no spouse or children, she couldn't even fulfill her life goal of singing. Distressed and worried, as you can well imagine, she lived in a tiny one-bedroom apartment three or four flights above the street level in a big city. With her mother gone, she lived alone in an old, run-down, apartment building where only old people on Social Security usually live.

One day, as Hazel was on her way out, she saw a young hippie-looking guy moving into one of the small tenements. He had a full beard and long hair. When she returned, all of her friends were talking about the new tenant. "We're in real trouble now," said one lady. "Once these tough-looking characters move in, they always take over!" And all the old folks living in the apartment building started taking extra precautions, just in case the stranger was a thief. Many even put extra locks on their windows and doors. Nobody trusted him.

This went on for several weeks. Then one night Hazel came in later than usual. She entered the lobby very quietly, so she wouldn't disturb any of the other tenants. After climbing two flights of stairs, she saw a suspicious-looking man in the hallway. Instead of screaming or running back down the stairs, she began to sing! In her own off-key way she sang the first words that came to her. "When you walk through a storm hold your head up high and don't be afraid of the dark." That's the only song she could remember and she wasn't even sure if the words were right. She sang on: ". . . Hold your head up high and you'll never walk alone. Walk on, walk on, with hope in your heart and you'll never walk alone." By this time she had reached her apartment. So she quickly opened the door and locked it securely, listening at the door for some kind of sound. She heard nothing, so she went to bed, grateful that she had made it safely to her place.

The next morning she saw a torn, crumpled piece of paper under her door. It was from the rough-looking young man that everyone feared. This is what it said: "I don't know who you are, but thank you for singing to me last night. I was ready to cash in—to commit suicide—but then you started to sing: 'When you walk through a storm hold your head up high and you'll never walk alone.' I want you to know that you saved my life. I'm going to another city where I know I can find the job I need. Thank you. Good-bye."

The power of a smile or the words of encouragement! Only God can say how valuable it is! Any impossibility thinker can count the seeds in an apple. Only God can count the apples in a seed! Only God knows how powerful your gift is.

Do the Dogs Like It?

A sales manager developed a new dog food. All the proteins, minerals, fats, and carbohydrates were included in the product. The company came out with a brand-new package and a national advertising program that included full-page ads and ingenious commercials. But after six months, the sales (which had started slowly) had finally dwindled to nothing. So the chairman of the board called all the district sales managers together in a major convention in Chicago. "What's wrong?" he asked. "Look at the beautiful full-page ads we have in national magazines. Look at the expensive commercials on television." Then he held up a box of the dog food and pointed to the back of the box. He read the contents and admired the beautiful packaging. "The cost is even lower than our competitors," he added. "Now tell me why you people aren't selling this dog food!" You could hear a pin drop. Then someone in the back of the room slowly came to his feet and said, "Sir, the dogs don't like it!"

The secret of success is not to sit in an expensive leather chair in a plush office and dream up your dreams. The secret of success is to find the need and fill it, to find a hurt and heal it, to find somebody with a problem and offer to help solve the problem.

The End Becomes a Bend

I remember when Mrs. Schuller, the children, and I came from the Midwest to California. We came across a mountain ridge and stopped to view the great valley beyond. The road stretched as straight as an arrow, for as far as we could see. But as we came closer and closer to the mountain ridge, it looked like the road stopped dead. But we didn't stop and turn around—we kept on going. And sure enough, twenty miles down that straight road, we saw that the road gradually curved. And as we followed the curve, it became a pass through the mountains.

That's the way God deals with us! You get started, even though you see a huge mountain range that makes it impossible to see beyond. You just keep on going, and at the right moment, the end becomes a bend!

Kyle, I Love You

An elder of our church named John Joseph shared this story with us at devotions the other night. John began by explaining that his wife and three daughters were back East. "I love my children and my wife. I miss them when we're separated—even for a little while. So we talk on the phone every night. One night my wife called me, and while we were talking, she told me Kyle, my nine-year-old daughter, wanted to talk to me.

"Kyle got on the line and said, 'Oh, Dad, I'm having such a wonderful time.' 'Kyle,' I said, 'it's so good to hear your voice. I . . .' I started to say, 'I love you.' But before I could say the words, she interrupted. 'I had such a wonderful time at the fair today, Daddy. It was so beautiful!' Again, as she paused, I tried to tell her, 'Kyle, I love you.' But again she interrupted, 'I'm so excited! I won the trophy, Dad.' And she proceeded to tell me all about the trophy. Once more I tried to tell her how important she is to me, how much I love her. But Kyle never gave me the chance. She interrupted once more and then said cheerily, 'Mom wants to talk to you again,' and handed the phone back to my wife.

"I was so depressed after that phone call I nearly cried. I wanted to say so desperately, 'Kyle, I love you. Kyle, I'm praying for you today.' I wanted to tell her, but she couldn't hear a word I said because, you see, Kyle is stone-deaf.

"It made me feel terrible to think my little Kyle couldn't hear what I wanted to say to her, until I realized that God has this problem with His children all the time. We're always in a hurry. And by nature, we're often stone-deaf to God's voice. When we pray, we do all the talking. God doesn't have a chance to say anything."

But God has a word for you. He has a plan for your life that will reflect His awesome, limitless love for you. All we have to do is listen.

A Report From "The International Psychological Convention"

Several years ago at the International Psychological Convention in Paris, France, I was involved in a fascinating seminar. A report was made of a study that was first begun approximately thirty years ago by graduate students at Johns Hopkins University. These students were told by their professor to go to the most emotionally, economically, and culturally deprived inner-city ghetto to analyze and document the lives of two hundred selected young men between the ages of twelve and sixteen. When they had completed their analysis of the subjects' economic, social, and cultural environment, they were to make a prediction based upon this data as to where these boys would be twenty-five years down the road.

When this portion of the study was completed, the graduate students predicted that of the 200 boys, 196 would spend at least some time in jail. I found that to be an incredibly gloomy prediction.

Twenty-five years later, another group of graduate students were assigned to find the 200 boys and check on the predictions. Eventually they found 180 of the 200. Of those they were able to locate, they discovered that only 6 of the 180 had ever spent any time at all in jail. The predictions of the previous behavioral scientists were totally wrong!

The students were then challenged to discover why, given the negative social environment which surrounded these young men during their formative years, they had not behaved as predicted. The students interviewed the men and asked them what was the most positive influence in their lives. Seventy-five percent of those questioned said the most positive influence in their lives was a teacher. Again and again one name emerged—the name of a woman teacher.

The students sought out the woman and found her in a retirement home. When they told her the results of the study she replied, "Is that right?"—not at all surprised. "How did you communicate with these young men, and what values did you impart in them? Did you have a specific strategy?" the students asked. "No, no," the old lady said shaking her head. Then slowly she smiled. "I just loved those boys," she replied. "I just loved those boys. That's all."

There's no force in the world as strong as the life-changing influence of a person who truly loves you. I've experienced that from Jesus Christ.

Dream Risky Dreams

She was a beautiful young girl, not more than twenty-one years old. She came to me this past week for counseling and guidance. She told me about a marvelous new friendship she has with this great guy. "You know, our relationship is so wonderful," she said. "We have such fun together. We can talk about anything and feel comfortable. And we both share the same love for God.

"But you know," she continued, "I'm afraid that

this relationship we share is leading somewhere seri-ous. I look around and see the unhappy marriages and the divorces, and I don't know if I should dare to believe I could be married in our kind of world.''

"As I see you and listen to you, do you know what I think about?" I asked her. "No," she replied.

"First of all, let me tell you that I've been a pastor for twenty-nine years. In those twenty-nine years I have married and baptized a lot of people, and con-ducted a lot of funerals. When I look at you and listen to you, I can see funerals.''

"Funerals!" she exclaimed in astonishment. "Yes," I replied. "I don't know how many dozens of times I have conducted a funeral for a man in his seventies or eighties. And as I walked the widow from the cemetery back to her car, she would look at me and say, 'You know, Reverend, I first met him when I was a teenager. Oh, we used to have so much fun. But secretly I wondered, *Can it last?* Then he asked me to marry him. I was so unsure of myself at first, but I said yes. And still I wondered, *Can it last?*

" 'Oh, we had our share of troubled times, but we grew together and learned to love each other even more. And before I knew it, we were celebrating our twenty-fifth wedding anniversary. We were so very happy that, in the midst of celebrating, I thought to myself, *Can it last?* And then, not long ago, we celebrated our forty-sixth year together. The children were all there, and we had such a wonderful time. And I thought to myself, *I'm so in love; how long can it last?* We were married forty-six years, and they were forty-six of the most beautiful, fulfilling years any person could ever hope for. He was such a good man. And we loved each other more with each passing year.' ''

As I studied the face of the young girl sitting across from me, I said, "When you describe your young man, I can suddenly see you when you're eighty years old, and you're saying to your pastor, 'You know, we had such a great relationship when we were teenagers. We shared so many wonderful things together and had so much fun. Then we got married, and we were so happy that we wondered, *How long can it last?* Yes, we had our share of tears and of growing times, but we've shared over forty years of joy. He was such a good man, and we loved each other all our lives together.' "

It takes courage to dream risky dreams. It can be seen in a young bride going to the altar, or in the groom who makes a commitment. They're people who dare to commit themselves to a dream, regardless of the risk they take, and it's beautiful.

Be Supportive

Yesterday I called on a lady in the hospital. "They say I'm terminal. They're not even giving me chemotherapy anymore. Everything has failed," she said. "Mary Lou," I soothed, "if what they mean by that is correct, the word is not terminal, it's *transitional.* You're not going to die; you're going through a transition." "But everything seems so hopeless," she persisted. Taking her hands in mine, I assured her, "When everything else fails, get ready to meet God, because that's when God steps in. He's always there. He never fails. This isn't an end for you; it's a beginning." And then she smiled at me and squeezed my hand and said, "Thank you. That helps."

For a brief moment I had the most wonderful feeling. I had been her supportive beam.

It's important that you take the time to get involved and become that supportive beam, that lift, that so many people need. When you become that kind of person, life becomes more exciting than you can imagine!

You Are Brilliant!

The head of a well-known company decided to test the creativity of average people, so he selected ten men from one of his factories. They were noneducated people at the bottom of the corporate ladder. The president led them into the executive headquarters and told them to sit in the big leather chairs around the huge board table. After they all sat down, he stood before them and explained why they had been chosen. "I have observed you people for some time now, and it has come to my attention that you all have remarkable gifts of creativity. This is why I have called you together today. Our company is facing a problem, and I believe that you ten men can come up with a solution." He explained all of the details and then left the room for a few hours, a little cynical of the whole idea. When he returned, he discovered they had found a solution.

It was in that meeting that a great breakthrough was made. They had found an answer to the problem that his top corporate research and development personnel had overlooked! The average "bottom-of-the-ladder person" is potentially as creatively brilliant as the top executive who is sitting in the big office. The only drawback is that the person on the bottom doesn't *realize* he's brilliant and doesn't believe in his own ideas.

The executive appealed to the employees' pride! He appealed to their self-worth! This is how he explains it: "Every person is creative! They only have to believe it. When I told the men they were smart, they believed it! They came up with a solution, because they were not informed enough to know that the suggestion they made couldn't be done. So, they came up with an idea that the rest of us never seriously considered because in our minds it was technologically impossible. And when they came up with the idea, we established it as a goal and solved the problem!"

Every human being has virtually equal creative possibilities. But why isn't the average person more creative? One simple reason: They don't *think* they are creative. Nobody's every told them they're creative, so they have never tried to be. There are incredible ideas that come to their minds once in a while, but they don't do anything about them. And then, years later, they read that somebody else did something with the idea. And they say to themselves, "I thought about that; why didn't I do something about it?"

I don't suppose there is one fact that I can try to communicate to you that is more important than this next sentence: "All of you are brilliant!" That's a *fact*. All of us have incredibly creative potential, because all creative ideas come from God.

Believe in Yourself

The glass elevator in our Tower of Hope was inspired by the El Cortez Hotel in San Diego. The owners of the elegant hotel decided they needed additional elevators, so they hired a group of architects and engineers to figure out the best location, both in terms of appearance and cost. If they put the elevators inside the hotel, they would have to cut a hole in all the floors. What a mess! Plaster dust would be everywhere.

As the planners stood in the lobby deliberating over the placement of these elevators, a janitor overheard the conversation. All he could think of was the mess the hotel was going to be in while all this reconstruction was going on inside. And the more he thought about it, the braver he got, until finally he went up to the group of men and said, "Why don't you put the elevators outside the building?" Nobody had thought of that! The professionals listened and the idea clicked in their imagination. "Why not?" they said. "It's never been done before, but let's try and see how we could do it." So the elevators were built outside the El Cortez Hotel and since then, many well-known buildings have done the same!

Common people are brilliant if they'll only believe in their own ideas! I don't care who you are. I don't care how poor you are. I don't care how illiterate you are. I don't care how educated you are. I don't care what your race is. I don't care where you are on the economic ladder. You have the same basic brain as any other human being! Believe in yourself.

No Idea Is Perfect!

Remember John Steinbeck's famous story "The Pearl"? A man found a beautiful pearl, but it had one tiny flaw. He thought if he could just remove that little imperfection, the pearl would be the biggest and the most priceless one in the world. So he peeled off the first layer, but the flaw was still there. Then he took off the next layer, thinking it would disappear, but the flaw remained. He continued to take off each layer, until finally he had no pearl. The flaw was gone now, but so was the beautiful prize.

No idea is perfect! No idea is without its problems. God sets it up that way in order for us to be humble enough to seek His help all along the way.

The Faith of Stanley Reimer

Every Sunday morning I see a very special person sitting about ten rows back on the right side of the auditorium. His name is Stanley Reimer, and he's an elder on our church board. I'll never forget the day when I received the tragic news that Stanley had a heart attack. Stan was a chemist with a large company, and the news was that he had a twenty-two-minute cardiac arrest. Twenty-two minutes! You know what that means. There was a considerable amount of time when oxygen did not reach the brain. And if Stan survived, he would probably be a vegetable all of his life. They managed to get him breathing again, but he was in a death coma. He was placed in the intensive care unit immediately, and his body was breathing on its own, but he was still in a coma. There was no sign of life other than the breathing that was going on. The neurosurgeon told Stan's wife that there was no hope. "If he keeps breathing, he'll be a vegetable all his life. He'll never close his eyes. They'll be open in a death stare as you see now. Totally, a vegetable."

I rushed to the hospital as soon as I could, praying the whole time. "God," I prayed, "what will I say?" What will I say to his wife? And then I remembered what I was taught in theological seminary: *Someday, as a pastor, you may be talking to someone in a death coma. When that happens, only think life! Only talk life! If you're ever at the bedside of a presumably dying patient, and he's in a coma so deep that no response is indicated, talk life! He may lack the power to move his lips or manifest a physical indication that he is hearing, but his subconscious may hear! And you must not place a negative thought in that mind!*

So I went into the intensive-care unit where he was lying, and there was Billie, his wife, standing at the bedside, tears streaming down her face. My once outgoing friend looked like a statue. He couldn't move—dead for all practical appearances—but he was breathing. His eyes were wide open. I put my arm around Billie and prayed with her. Then I took hold of his hand and softly said, "Stanley, I know you cannot talk. I know you cannot respond, but I know that deep down within you, you can hear me. I'm Bob Schuller. I've just come from church where everyone is praying for you. And Stanley, I've got news for you. You had a bad heart attack, but you are going to recover. You are going to live, and it's going to be a long battle. It's going to be hard, but you're going to make it!''

And at that point I had one of the most moving experiences of my life. A tear rolled out of my friend's eye. He understood! No smile, no quiver of a lip, but a tear rolled out of his eye. The doctors couldn't believe it! That was over a year ago and today Stanley is able to speak full sentences, he can hear, and his faculties are becoming normalized.

A miracle? Remember:

"If you have faith as a grain of mustard seed you can say to your mountain, 'Move' and nothing will be impossible.''

In the darkest time, tell yourself that faith will move the mountain! Faith will help and faith will heal, but you must not give up believing.

Run, Patty, Run!

Patty Wilson was thirteen years old when she discovered she was an epileptic. Her dad did everything he could to convince her that she shouldn't have a negative self-image because of this condition. He knew that she would encounter discrimination, and he didn't want to see her get hurt. One day Patty's dad was driving to work, when he saw a man running along the sidewalk in runner's shoes and clothes, but there was something strange about his feet. They looked like the hoofs of a horse! Mr. Wilson did a

double take and threw his car into reverse. He later
found out that the man was born with no feet, and
his custom-made running shoes looked like the hoofs
of a horse. That one incident inspired Patty's dad to
run! Mr. Wilson thought, "If he can run, so can I!"
And it was at this point that he vowed to teach Patty
that she was normal. And he was going to make her
believe it!

As Patty watched her dad run each morning, she
became interested and was soon running alongside of
him. Day after day, week after week, month after
month, you could see the father-daughter team running through the neighborhood. Then Patty was inspired with a dream. *How can I encourage the world
to treat epileptics like normal people?* she wondered.
She asked her dad what the women's record for long-
distance running was and set a goal to break it. She
decided she'd run from Orange County to San Diego,
100 miles; to Las Vegas, 300 miles; and then to San
Francisco, 500 miles. These were her major goals.

She trained for a year to make it. And she said,
"At the end of my sophomore year, I'll run from
Orange County to Portland, Oregon [1,000 miles]."
She didn't stop there! "At the end of my junior
year," she determined, "I will run from Orange
County to Saint Louis, Missouri [2,000 miles]. And
at the end of my senior year, when I graduate from
high school, I'll celebrate by running from Orange
County across the United States of America to Washington, D.C. I want to shake hands with the President at the White House."

How's that for big thinking by a teen-age epileptic
girl? Talk about possibility thinking! Well, she tried
and last year she made it! She ran 500 miles from

Orange County to San Francisco, California. And this year, at the end of her sophomore year, she was ready to try for Portland, Oregon—1,000 miles. And when the event was to occur, her high-school classmates had a big paper banner stretched across the street, and they wrote in red, sloppy ink—RUN, PATTY, RUN! There were some ceremonies, and I said a prayer. I even placed my medallion around her neck!

What an exciting moment when Patty ran through and ripped the paper banner! She went running down the road, on the way towards the coast, on the way to Portland, Oregon, 1,000 miles. Driving behind at a safe distance was her mother, a licensed vocational nurse, with medication in case she had a seizure. And tacked on the back of the van were the words: PATTY WILSON, WORLD'S WOMEN'S LONG-DISTANCE RUNNER RECORD-HOLDER—RUNNING FROM CALIFORNIA TO OREGON. We followed her every day with our prayers. She did great until 28 miles later, when she cracked a bone in her foot. Her parents took her to the emergency room of the hospital, praying that it wasn't serious. Doctors X-rayed her foot and concluded that it was fractured. The doctor said, "Patty, you'd better not run, because if you do, you may have permanent injury." Patty knew that there were thousands of people that were expecting her to run and complete the adventure. "Doctor," she said, "if you wrapped it tight, don't you think I could keep running?" "Yes, you might do it," he explained, "but you'll get terrible blisters." "That's just water under the skin," Patty enthused. "My mother's a nurse. Couldn't she take the liquid out with a syringe?" "Yes," the doctor replied. "Just be careful." So Patty tightly wrapped her foot up and went back onto the road. It hurt! But she kept on running —*500* miles, *600, 700, 800, 900, 1,000!*

They decided to take the coastal route, not stopping to think that it was 300 miles farther. One thousand, 1,100, 1,200, 1,300—and when they were about a mile outside of Portland, Oregon, the governor got his running suit on and ran with her the last mile. The entire city was out to greet her, and what a welcome she got! She endured the pain! There was no permanent injury to her foot, so she's in great shape. And Patty's already talking about running across the U.S.A. And when she makes it, you'll hear about her!

Stop and think. *How?* Have you been as faithful to your dream as Patty Wilson has been to hers?

Faith will never fail you—unless you give up! Patty didn't give up! And she's still climbing! Today's impossibilities are tomorrow's possibilities! Keep on keeping on! Believe in yourself!

We Need You

If you've taken a cruise on an ocean liner, you've had the thrill of first catching sight of the shore. When you come into a new port, you see a huge mass of floating hotels with their precious cargo of hundreds and hundreds of persons and their property. A tugboat brings the ship in slowly and carefully, until it's right against the pier. Now the ship has to be tied firmly to the dock, or the gangplank will tip and topple with the slightest swell of the water. The ship has to be tied tightly! And if you've been past the dock or pier, you've seen these huge ropes thicker than your arm that hold the ship tight against the dock. The crew doesn't throw the big rope onto the shore, for it's too heavy. A sailor at the bow with another at the stern holds in his hand a little ball. He throws the ball onto the dock, and trailing behind it is a thin line, like a kite string. Somebody on the dock picks up that ball and pulls in the kite string. And tied to the thin string is a little rope, the size of a clothesline. When he gets hold of it, he and his crewmen can pull the boat to the dock.

So the great liner unloads its cargo and is ready to set sail again. Who made it possible? The captain? Yes. But it was also that thin little line that was the key for all of the maneuvering. The captain, the tugboats, and those who work on the pier would fail if it weren't for that thin string tied to a rope. The crew can keep the ship running, but when it gets to the bottom line, it takes a thin thread to make a journey a success.

You Are Important

Many of you think you're not important; you don't see life in its whole perspective. We have a furnace in our home that has a little pilot light. That small flame has to be faithful in order for the big furnace to work. The pilot ignites the bigger furnace, which heats the entire house. Friends visiting my home on a cold day might comment on the comfortable temperature inside the house, but nobody ever compliments the pilot light. Nobody thinks about the poor little flame. I have news for you. In every successful institution and enterprise, there is at least one person who is the pilot light. He or she throws on the big furnace to make things happen.

I went to Hope College, in Holland, Michigan, a great institution with very high academic standards. When I was there, the president of the college was Dr. Irwin Lubbers. Every so often I would see him cut across campus on his way to a meeting. He would rarely talk to the students, for he seemed to have so many things on his mind. In fact, there was only one person that I ever saw him stop and talk to, and that was the gardener. Now I knew that young man. He had suffered from a childhood illness and was limited in his mental capacity. Sometimes I'd be sitting on the lawn reading, when Dr. Lubbers would walk by and stop to talk with the man. They would laugh and shake hands, as if they were good friends. The college president always seemed to have a new spring in his step as he walked on. He was the furnace, and the gardener was the pilot light. Every institution has to have that kind of pilot light! You can be an inspiration to somebody!

The Inspiration for Mary Crowley

Mary Crowley, president of Home Interiors, a very prosperous business, was in Nassau, in the Bahamas, with her husband some years ago. It was a Sunday morning, so they decided to go to church. They found a local church filled with nearby citizens. There were all black people in the congregation. She tells the story of how the huge, silver-haired preacher, with a thundering voice and a rusty, gravelly tone, kept pounding home one theme to his people all morning. Talking to his people he bellowed out, "Be somebody! God never takes time to build a nobody. Everybody God creates is created to be *somebody*!"

That black preacher probably never knew what an inspiration he was to Mary Crowley. Little did he realize that he would be the one to inspire a woman to go back to the United States with that positive message: "*Be* somebody! God never takes time to create a nobody!" And she has been sharing that theme now until her organization reaches into every state in the country! Be somebody! God never takes time to create a nobody!

The Inspiration of George Truitt

When I was a theology student, I was assigned to write a term paper on a minister named George Truitt. At that time, I had never heard of him. I discovered that he had come to a tiny congregation in Dallas, Texas, and decided to spend his life in that church. He labored in his congregation for forty years, until it became one of the largest and the finest

Baptist churches in the world. I was so inpired by this story that I prayed then and there: "God, I'm a young man; lead me to some place where I can spend forty years and start a church from scratch." George Truitt was the pilot for this church. Now we, in turn, are inspiring others. You can be an inspiration to somebody if you have the right source—if you're set on the right course, and if you have the force behind you. Jesus Christ is the source of my inspiration. He said:

> "For the Scriptures declare that rivers of living water shall flow from the inmost being of anyone who believes in me."
>
> John 7:38 LB

The Saudi Problem

> It is the glory of God to conceal a thing. And it is the glory of kings to reveal it.
>
> Proverbs 25:2

Dr. Paul Harrison, one of the great surgeons of the twentieth century, spent most of his life in Saudi Arabia as a missionary for our church. I remember he used to tell of one tremendous problem the Arabs (who lived in bleak, sandy deserts) constantly had to deal with—the problem of keeping their sheep alive. It seemed that the sheep were constantly being poisoned by a black substance which oozed from the ground and swirled through the animals' watering holes. At that time, the Arabs didn't know that that black substance was of far greater value to them than their flocks of sheep. Unknowingly, they had discovered oil. *It is the glory of God to conceal a thing. And it is the glory of kings to reveal it.*

An American Success Story

Not long ago I had dinner with a remarkable man at his home in Miami, Florida. This man was born in a very tough neighborhood in Flint, Michigan. When I met with him, he said, "Doctor Schuller, you asked me what kind of neighborhood I lived in, how tough my gang was. Let me explain. Of my friends, eleven are dead. Five were murdered. And four are serving life sentences for murder." That man is, today, forty-three years of age. He showed me his hands. They had been scarred from innumerable street battles. Even today the carriage of his body still reflects the attitude of the street.

At eighteen he dropped out of high school with a *D* average. He met a young girl and soon married when she became pregnant. Their first child had barely been born when the young man's wife became pregnant once again. He had no idea how to support his new family and little hope for his marriage. Desperation drove him to seek help from a black marriage counselor.

After talking to him for a while and giving him some aptitude tests, the counselor said, "You should either be a mechanic or a salesman." So the young man enrolled in mechanic's trade school sponsored

by General Motors. Two weeks after he began working he looked at his grease-covered body and thought
with despair, "I just can't do this for the rest of my
life!" While walking home, he passed a used-car lot.
He wished he could have money for a car and wondered, "Could I be a salesman?"

The manager of the lot asked, "You, looking for a
car. You got any money?" "Maybe," the man
replied. "Maybe I'm looking for a job." The man
gave him a job working on the lot for forty dollars a
week. His first week on the lot, the young man
astounded everyone, including himself, by selling fifteen cars.

He'd not been at the lot very long when one of his
customers offered him a job selling furniture for a
small base salary plus commission. At the end of his
first year on the job he had a pregnant wife, two
children, and a gross income of twenty-eight thousand dollars. He was not yet nineteen years old. His
second year he earned forty-two thousand dollars.

At twenty-two, he borrowed ten thousand dollars
from his father (who had mortgaged his house) and
set up his own furniture store. During his first thirty
days in business he sold two hundred thousand
dollars in gross sales, fifty thousand of which was his
net profit. By the end of that year, he netted $1
million. He retired at the age of twenty-eight with a
personal fortune of $15 million.

Today he spends his time working on the boards of
directors of various Catholic institutions and chari-
table organizations. In addition to being a father to
nine children and a grandfather, he's using his
energies to inspire people who are looked upon as
hopeless punks to "believe you can do something and

be somebody." My friend, you have the possibilities within you you haven't dared to believe.

"Follow More Closely"

Recently I was scheduled to speak to a group of bishops and leaders in the Roman Catholic Church as well as leaders of the Protestant churches in New Orleans. Because I had so much work to do, I booked the 12:30 flight to New Orleans, which would arrive at 6:00 P.M.—one hour before the dinner was to begin. I figured that if the plane arrived at 6:00, that would give me a half hour to be briefed. I thought I had it timed perfectly.

The problem was that the plane ran into a problem in Los Angeles and didn't leave on time. Fifteen, then thirty minutes passed. Finally, forty-five minutes later, the plane took off, and I landed in New Orleans about twelve minutes to 7:00. The two principal officials of the event were waiting for me when I stepped off the plane, along with a police officer. We left the airport, and I climbed into the waiting car. The police officer led the way in his car. All of a sudden, the light on the police car started turning and the siren blew. I was soon aware that we were having a police escort.

You know, that's really kind of an ego trip. Having a police escort really made me feel important. And I must confess, it's a lot better feeling having the siren ahead of you than behind you!

The policeman was leading the way down the ex-

pressway and everybody was pulling to the side to let
us pass. Then suddenly the police car pulled over to
the curb. Our driver didn't know what that meant,
and we were still some minutes from our destination,
so we kept on driving. Soon, however, he pulled beside us. Through his megaphone I could hear him
say, "You've got to follow me more closely." Boy,
we had to hang right in there behind him, as he led
the way.

In the same way, God moves ahead of us. He
thinks bigger than either you or I can think. He
knows you have far more potential than you give
yourself credit for. He has more, far more, faith in
you than you have in yourself. And your job is to
"follow more closely."

Look for the Rainbow

I suppose the most successful publishing venture in
America outside of the Bible is the *Old Farmer's
Almanac*. It's a super success and has been for
almost a hundred years. In July, 1883, the editor was
finishing the final draft for the year's almanac. He
had worked all the way into the following year, esti-
mating what the weather would be every day from
January through July 12, 1884. But as the accomplished writer neared completion, he grew tired. So
he thought he'd pick up the next day with July 13,
1884.

Just as he was about to go home, a boy came running in and exclaimed, "You can't go! The printer is

demanding the remaining pages tonight—all the way through July thirteenth. You must stay and finish!" "I've had it," the editor said. "Just write in some kind of temperature and weather for July thirteenth. Frankly, your guess is as good as mine." And he forgot all about it.

So the young boy wrote in his weather forecast: "Wind, hail, and snow." When the almanac finally came out and was being distributed, the editor looked through it and saw what the boy had written. He was furious! He called the boy in and said, "This is outrageous! We're barely making it, and now this is going to ruin us. There's no way there can be wind, hail, and snow on July thirteenth!" Well, on July 13, 1884, there was wind, hail, and snow, like never before and never since. And when the United States read that the *Old Farmer's Almanac* had predicted it ten months before, their reputation soared overnight to make them a national success!

Sometimes we think that everything that happens to us is bad news. Remember this: Good news will always follow bad news! There is a rainbow that rises out of the storm. You may have to wait a while, but good news always follows bad news. That's why you need a connection with God through Jesus Christ, and if you have that, you may have problems, but you can make it!

Take a Look at Your Good Times

Look at what you have left. Don't look at what you've lost. Look at your good times—don't look at your bad times.

I had lunch with a very good friend last week to check up on his health, because he's been very ill. I asked him how he was. "Oh, I'm terrific now," he answered. Six months ago he was in very bad shape. We prayed together often on the telephone. "You know, Bob," he shared, "there was a time when I was so sick that I thought every day was a bad day and every hour was a totally bad hour. Then one day I said to my wife, 'Honey, I haven't had five good minutes today.' 'That's not true,' she enthused, 'you just don't remember the good minutes.' And I thought to myself, 'She may be right!'

"The next day I went to the store and purchased a looseleaf notebook, so I could start my own personal diary. My plan was that any time in the course of the day when I felt good I would write it down. For instance, right after breakfast I said, 'The bacon tasted good.' That was a good experience so I wrote it down. At the end of the day, I looked at the good things that had happened. It really wasn't all bad after all! The next day I did the same thing. Now I have a very thick diary!" In the worst time a lot of good things can happen!

Inflate Your Possibilities

The other day I read about a man who was marooned on an island a year ago. According to the anecdote, he was not rescued until the year 2000. The first thing he did when he returned to civilization was to go to a pay phone, where he dropped in a coin and called his broker.

"Hey, I'm back," he said. "You know, of course, I've been gone for twenty years. Tell me, how did my General Motors stock do?"

"Oh," the broker said, "It's done incredibly well. It's now worth nine million dollars."

"How about my house?" exclaimed the man breathlessly, "What is it worth?"

"Oh, your house is worth about two and a half million," the broker replied.

The man was rejoicing over his good fortune, when the operator broke in. "I'm sorry," she said, "your three minutes are up. Please deposit one million dollars."

None of us knows what the future will bring. We know we're caught up in economic inflation—but will your possibilities also inflate? Will your personal development also inflate? It can—if you practice right thinking, believe, pray, and live the kind of life God has planned for you. You, too, can say, "I can do all things through Christ which strengtheneth me" (Philippians 4:13 KJV).

Listen: Your Key to Harmony

When I was in high school, I sang in a male quartet. Later, when I entered college, I made a point of joining another quartet. We made many concert tours throughout the United States. In fact, I made my first trip to California when I was in the Hope College traveling, touring quartet. I'll never forget my high-school music teacher saying, "Boys, the key to a good male quartet is equal balanced harmony. All voices *must* be equally balanced!" Then she went on to explain how to obtain harmony.

"Listen to yourself sing, but also listen to the other voices on each side of you," she explained. "If the voices on either side of you are a little louder than you, you know that you have to sing a little louder. If you hear yourself louder than you hear those on each side of you, then you are singing too loud; tone down a little. All you have to do is use your ears! Make sure that you don't sing louder or softer than the voices around you. *Listen!*"

I have discovered that that is also an important principle for interpersonal relationships. The tragedy is most people listen to their own will. They listen to their own wishes—to their own desires. They hear the inner voice of their own selfish desires so strongly, that when somebody else comes along with a suggestion or an idea, a request or an appeal, they really don't hear it. They only hear what satisfies their own desires. Then they wonder why they fail, or why things fall apart, or why disharmony moves in. They wonder why they are not happy, and why they are not enthusiastic, why they are not sparkling and twinkling. Disharmony produces gloom. Harmony produces sparkle. The key is listening to what others are trying to say to you. And most important—this listening must be with regularity.

The Place for Negativity

A very negative-thinking minister was given a promotion. He was to leave his pastorate and become a bishop. He was replaced by a young, positive, enthusiastic fellow who had just graduated from theological seminary. This young minister entered the stiff, stodgy, and stuffy old church with great ideas. He initiated some recreational programs and led a more liberal service on Sunday mornings. When his predecessor heard what was happening to his old pastorate he became distressed. The bishop couldn't see his previous church led down the road to destruction, so he pulled his rank of authority and demanded an opportunity to return to his old pulpit.

The bishop came with determination to straighten out the congregation—to correct this impetuous, impulsive, ridiculously progressive and ultraliberal successor. He stood before the congregation and berated the young pastor. It was a very embarrassing and sordid scene. When he was finished, with flushed face, the humiliated minister came up to the pulpit to conclude the service. With his head hung in remorse he addressed the people. "I'm sorry; I can make mistakes." Then pointing to his beloved congregation, he said, "You can make mistakes." And turning to the bishop he said, "And the bishop can make mistakes." There was complete silence as he continued. "I can sin. You can sin. And the bishop can sin. I could go to hell, you could go to hell, and the bishop can go to hell." There is a lot of negativity in religion!

A lot of religion can go to hell because that is exactly where it is! That is the truth! What is hell? Hell is a state of being separated from God. Hell is a state when we are not consumed by His love and by the awareness of His Presence. Whatever hell is, wherever hell is, this we know: There can be no hell if you stand in the heart of the presence of the love of God.

"He Was Leaning Against the Wind"

I was in Boston recently and the wind was blowing fiercely. It reminded me of the experience of Bill Stidger, a student at the Boston University. Bill always walked to school early in the morning. One morning he noticed a large group of people gathered at the base of a skyscraper being built, so he moved into the crowd. "What's happening?" he asked a man with a hard hat who looked like a foreman. "One of the workers just got killed," the workman replied. And Bill Stidger, a student for the ministry, asked, "How did it happen?" "The fool," the foreman angrily answered, "he was leaning against the wind!'' And then with tears in his eyes, he added, ''When I hired him last week I distinctly said, 'Don't lean against the wind!' ''

''What does he mean?'' Bill asked another hard-hat standing nearby. ''What does he mean, *leaning against the wind?*'' ''Oh,'' the other steelworker said, ''here in Boston there is always a steady breeze in the morning. A firm, pressurized wind comes off the ocean and leans against the skeleton of this building. So when we work up there, it's so easy to lean against the wind. But about nine o'clock in the morning, the wind always cuts off. And always without any warning! This new guy had just come from Indianapolis. He was used to working on a highrise, but he's not used to working in Boston. He was leaning against the wind, and when the wind cut off, he fell.''

If you are down on living, you are leaning against the wind. Don't lean against the wind; lean upon a solid rock. Lean against Jesus Christ.

''Every one then who hears these words of mine and does them will be like a wise man who built his house upon the rock; and the rain fell, and the floods came, and the winds blew and beat upon that house, but it did not fall, because it had been founded on the rock.''

Matthew 7:24, 25 RSV

How to Succeed in Tough Times

I want to share with you the story of a very dear friend of mine who, incidentally, prefers to remain anonymous. He was a salesman during the Great Depression in the early 1930s—a time when salesmen as a whole weren't doing well at all. One night at a sales meeting a fellow salesman told him the story of a man who had made a lot of money with the Coca-Cola Company. "Did you hear about the guy who went to Coca-Cola with an idea which would vastly expand the sales of their product?" he asked. "No," someone in the group answered. "What do you mean?"

"Well," the man continued, "this guy wrote to Coca-Cola and told them he had an idea that could be enormously profitable to their company. All he asked was a fraction of one percent of the gross sales realized as a result of his idea. At first he was ignored, but he kept badgering everyone so consistently that finally management agreed to see him and hear him out.

"Do you know what the idea was?" the man asked. "He told those smart executives that they would multiply sales if they would sell only bottled Coca-Cola."

Up until that time Coca-Cola had been sold only in large containers to drugstores. Nobody had ever thought of putting it in bottles and selling it to grocery stores and other retail outlets. Coca-Cola agreed to his terms, tried the idea, and it was so successful that the man made multiple millions.

My friend went home that night and thought about what he had heard. The next day he took his car to a service station to get oil put into it. The only way to get oil was for the service-station attendant to pump it out of huge drums, and then pour it into the car. *I wonder if I could bottle automobile oil?* my friend mused. *No,* he thought. *If the bottles broke, that would really be a mess. I wonder if I could put oil in cans and sell it that way?*

He went to a friend in Pennsylvania who owned an oil refinery that was refining more oil than could be marketed. His friend agreed to allow him to have the excess oil for a reasonable percentage of the profits. Then my friend went to a can company and made arrangements with them to purchase some cans. Finally he went to the A&P and said to the marketing manager, "How would you like to expand your retail sales enormously by selling car oil in cans?" All he asked as payment was seventy-five dollars for each freight carload of canned oil that was sold. In the middle of the Great Depression, this man made millions of dollars. He used that money as the basis for establishing what is today an incredible financial empire. And he's given millions of dollars to numerous great causes. In the worst of times, somebody is going to get a bright idea!

"*A*/440"

When Jesus becomes Lord of our lives, He becomes our solid, single integrating force—our "*A*/440."

Let me explain: Suppose that a concert was planned featuring the three greatest pianists in the world, perhaps Van Cliburn, Liberace, and Rubinstein. Each will play in a different city—one in New York, one in Tokyo, and one in Paris—and the three will be simultaneously broadcast via international satellite. In America, and around the world, viewers could see and hear these three great artists playing the same composition at the same moment on a triple screen. Such an event is technically possible.

However, we encounter one problem: How do you make sure all pianos are tuned exactly alike? You can't, very practically, get all three pianos on a plane, tune them and then ship them to three different concert halls. Could you tune them using a taped recording of one piano as the basis for tuning the remaining two? The variable for error is still too great. How could it be done? By tuning the three pianos by $A/440$ above middle C. The A above middle C is tuned to produce 440 vibrations per second when it is struck. This measure will be the same in Tokyo, Paris, and New York City—$A/440$ is an absolute, international measure in relation to music.

When the angels appeared at Christmastime, what they were really announcing was the arrival of God's greatest gift to the world—an international standard by which we could tune our lives. Whatever your race, culture, religious belief (or lack of it)—you, without exception—need an internationally valid moral, spiritual, and emotional standard that can determine your human values. Who do you tune your life by? The moral standards and human values of others? If so, that's perfectly normal. But it is probably a basic reason why you're not happy.

Can you imagine how an orchestra would sound if each musician was pursuing his own ego trip and said, "My pitch is perfect. I'll tune my instrument by my own ear." The result would be a maddening cacophony. Instead the oboe is tuned to $A/440$. (The oboe is chosen for the purity of its notes. More than any other instrument, its sound is free from overtones.) And the remaining instruments take their pitch from the oboe.

Until Jesus was born, the world was like an orchestra without an $A/440$. Jesus became the integrating force upon whom we can form our basic value system. Before Him, there was no standard for all human beings. No other religious leader in history ever said, "I am the Way, the Truth and the Life." No other human being claimed to be humanity's guiding North Star—the moral, emotional, and spiritual $A/440$ above middle C. Jesus is God's standard for every person for all time to come.

My Most Memorable Christmas

The other day someone asked, "Doctor Schuller, what is your most memorable Christmas?" "I think I can answer that," I replied, "and I don't think it will change during my lifetime. I can't imagine any Christmas more memorable than the Christmas of 1978." That was the year—and I shall never forget it—when our young daughter Carol, age thirteen, was thrown from a motorcycle on which she was a passenger. She sailed eighty-nine feet through the air and landed in a ditch where she almost died. My wife and I were on a mission in Korea when we got the news that the doctors were in the process of amputating her left leg.

Our plane flight home took twenty-two hours. I suppose I did more crying on that flight than I ever have in my entire life. When my wife and I arrived at my daughter's side, unable to think of adequate words of comfort, surprisingly enough, Carol began the conversation. "Dad," she said, "I think God has a special ministry for my life to help people who have been hurt as I have." She saw possibilities—positive ones—in tragedy! What a lift those words gave me. But we were just beginning what would prove to be a long, exhaustive battle. Carol's femur broke in four places and plunged through the thigh bone and into the ditch of an Iowa farm, next to a slaughterhouse. There it picked up a form of bacteria, which had previously been resistant to any known antibiotics.

The accident happened in July. In November, Carol went back into the hospital for surgery which would, hopefully, release muscles in her knee that might make her leg more usable. The doctor was so delighted when he opened her thigh and knee and discovered no pus pockets. But the hidden bacteria which, until that time had remained dormant, erupted like a prairie fire when exposed to the open air. Three days after surgery she was the sickest little girl I've ever seen.

Each passing day, the bacteria multiplied with increasing impatience. Carol's fever soared to 104 degrees and lingered there day after day, night after night. Her leg continued to swell and the infection raged out of control.

About that time we were blessed with a minor miracle. With no knowledge of my daughter's need, the Federal Drug Administration released, for the first time, an antibiotic that was declared significantly effective against that specific strain of bacteria Carol contracted while lying in that Iowa ditch. She was the first human being in Children's Hospital, Orange Country, California, to receive it. In a matter of hours after the first dosage, her temperature went down. Each successive culture reading showed fewer and fewer bacteria until, about three weeks before Christmas, a culture came back that showed no bacteria growth.

Lying in her hospital bed with the intravenous tubes still in her hands, Carol asked the visiting doctor, who was standing in for her own surgeon, when she would be released. "Will I be home for Christmas, doctor?" she asked. "I don't know," he replied cautiously. "Will I be able to get my new prosthesis? All I want for Christmas is my new fake foot," she chimed. "Well," the doctor cautioned, "I don't believe you can get it yet."

But when her doctor returned from his lecture trip to Spain, he checked her over. That same day Carol called me at my office. "Daddy, I have good news," she announced. "What is it?" I asked. "Doctor Masters is an angel," she exclaimed. "He said I can come home for Christmas!"

On December 16, a Saturday night, Carol was released from the hospital. I was told to stay home and await a surprise. My wife went to pick her up. I saw the lights of the car, as it rolled up the driveway. Then I saw the taillights go on as the brake pedal was pressed, and I ran to the front door. My wife opened the door and said, "Bob, you have to go back in and wait. Carol wants you to ' wait by the Christmas tree.''

So I waited nervously by the Christmas tree, counting the seemingly interminable seconds. Then I heard the front door open and the squeak of rubber on the wooden floor. I knew the sound came from the rubber tips of Carol's crutches. Then she stepped into the open door, ten feet away from my seat by the Christmas tree. She had gone straight from the hospital to the beauty parlor (typical girl) where she had had the most beautiful permanent. Then she stood with the most lovely curls framing her face. And I looked down and saw two shoes, two ankles, two legs —a beautiful girl. Carol got her new foot for Christmas. In my mind, *that* Christmas will always be the most memorable!

The White House Experience

Not long ago I was in the White House on a Wednesday and a Thursday. On Wednesday, I was invited by Mrs. Carter to attend a press conference which announced the launching of a national campaign, one which would announce and promote television programs for the deaf. A new technology has been developed which allows a deaf person to attach a small adaptor to the television set. When this is accomplished, this person can see the words spoken and sung by television personalities move across the bottom of the screen. Only on a television set fitted with this adaptor will the words appear. So if a person has impaired hearing or is totally deaf, he can read every word, just as a hearing person would read the subtitles of a foreign film. However, in order for the adaptor to be effective, the program must be specially produced. And that can be very expensive.

When we heard about the breakthrough some time ago, we immediately decided to implement the technique into our production of the "Hour of Power." In order to do this, we authorized the spending of an additional two thousand dollars per week to cover the expenses of this special facet of television production for the deaf. At the time we didn't realize it, but we were the first secular or sacred syndicated television program in the United States to use this special technique! So I was quite surprised when I got a letter from Mrs. Carter, inviting me to be with her at the White House for the press conference held in the East Room.

The next day I was invited to return to the East Room of the White House at the invitation of the President. There a group of national leaders met to talk about the problems of inflation and energy. First of all, Economic Adviser Charles Schultze spoke for about forty minutes on the problems of inflation. He urged the American people to be thrifty and pay off their credit cards.

I wanted to raise my hand and say, "I'm all for thrift. But may I suggest, sir, instead of taking a negative approach and saying, 'Don't use your charge card,' try a positive approach. Tell the people to put away as much as they can into savings accounts. Then declare that all of the interest paid to those savings accounts will be nontaxable income and eliminate the practice of allowing the interest on credit cards to be an income-tax deduction. Our tax feeds debt and fuels inflation.'' If the United States did that, then people would start saving and rise out of their poverty. That's what they do in Singapore and their inflation rate is only 4 percent and has been for the past 5 years. Place the emphasis on thrift and really reward the people who are saving positively by giving them incentives. Don't try to repress or restrict them.

However I didn't get a chance to voice my idea, and perhaps it's just as well. After Mr. Schultze finished speaking, Secretary Francis Duncan took his place at the podium and spoke about the energy crisis. He's right. We waste an incredible amount of energy. The President later told us that we spend 10 billion dollars every sixty minutes on imported oil. That statement really hit a responsive chord in me. We must conserve energy.

For years I've been urging my children to put the lights out, turn off the television or radio if they're not enjoying them. Even on business trips, I always remember to turn the lights out in my hotel room. Of course I'm not paying the bill, but that doesn't matter. The hotel management is getting this energy from the same ultimate source that everyone else is in America. We have to start conserving fuel and energy. Don't make unnecessary trips. Car pool whenever possible.

Then the President, too, urged Americans to be more thrifty and energy conscious. He suggested that we use solar energy. That statement immediately caught my attention, because we were sitting in the East Room on a bright sunny day with all the drapes drawn. Lights were blazing unnecessarily throughout the room! "Look," I wanted to say, "all the drapes are drawn. Why not let the natural sunlight illuminate the room?"

So when Mr. Schultze asked if there were any questions, I raised my hand. But he saw somebody else. I never got a chance to speak. Then Mr. Duncan finished his address and I raised my hand again. Although I was right in front of him, he didn't see me either. Then the President finished his speech with the words, "Everybody has to do their little part to save energy. Are there any questions?" I raised my hand and saw him look in my direction. But a congressman next to me popped up. He asked a question in the way typical with congressmen—he made a speech for five minutes! When his speech was finished, President Carter said, "I'm sorry, I have to leave."

The President walked out and Mr. Schultze and Mr. Duncan followed. Since I was right there in the center aisle, the very front seat, I followed the Secretary. Tapping him on the shoulder, I asked, "Hey, we've all got to conserve, right?" "Right," he answered emphatically. "Then I've got a question," I began. "I sat in the East Room for an hour and a half yesterday and for two and a half hours today. That's a total of four hours. Both days it was bright and sunny outside. And both days all the drapes were shut, darkening the room so all the lights had to be burning for four hours. Why didn't you use solar energy to light the place?"

He blushed and stammered. Finally he said, "Well, they need the room dark for television." Shaking my head I volunteered, "You know it's possible to get beautiful television production without any drapes drawn on the windows." Quite flustered he said, "I don't know," and pushed his way ahead and left in a hurry.

Friday night of that same week, I returned home and watched the President give his public address to the nation with regard to the United States's boycott of the Olympics in Moscow. Once again he was in the East Room. But do you know what? This time all the drapes were wide open! Now I'm not saying, of course, that I'm the reason for this change in White House procedure. But maybe they did decide to listen just a little bit. The point is that everybody can do their little bit to conserve energy.

Sealing the Windows of the Cathedral

Successful leaders must learn to manage time, money, energy, talent, and people. They also must learn to handle problems. The Crystal Cathedral, which was just constructed, is completely glazed. One of the final steps that had to be performed on the exterior was for each seam to be sealed where the windows come together. Everyone who was asked to bid on the job said it was impossible. Nobody could walk up and down on the steep sides of a slippery glass roof a football field in size. It would be impossible not to slide down.

Then one day a young man from Cupple's Company came to me and asked, "Doctor Schuller, did you see the little go-cart I invented?" It was a little device that would allow a man to sit in it and go back and forth along the roof and work the seams of the windows. "Anytime somebody says they can't do something," the young man said, "it simply means that they don't want to do it. You can do anything you want to. You just have to invent something new, that's all." He's a true possibility thinker!

Why You Need a Positive Church

Last week I was talking at length on the telephone with Dr. Lacy Hall, who is involved in the Stone-Brandel Center in Chicago, Illinois. He was telling me about an experiment they did at the center about three years ago. First, they recruited a large number of persons. Then they asked every person to keep a diary of their daily life—to record everything that came as an input into their mind or into their lives. He believed that we are the product of what comes into our lives, our minds, our hearts, and our emotional experiences. Dr. Hall wanted to find out what percentage of input into a human brain in the course of a day was positive and what percentage was negative.

Everyone was told to record everything that came into their brains in the course of a day for a year and a half. Their diaries began with the opening of the day. If they turned on the television set, they had to write down exactly what they watched—whether it was a newscast or a talk show, they had to log it into their diaries. Was the input positive or negative? If they worked, every encounter had to be recorded, whether positive or negative. If they listened to a radio station, read a certain newspaper or book, visited with family or friends, participated in any kind of entertainment or went to church—everything had to be documented.

After a year and a half, Dr. Hall said the data was collected, calculated, and computerized under controlled research at the Stone-Brandel Center in Chicago. The people who kept these diaries came up feeling discouraged or depressed all the time. Do you wonder why? Most people experienced 90 percent negative input. Only 10 percent of the thoughts that were fed to them, or the concepts that came into their life during the year and a half were positive! There were a few people who had a high percentage of positive input, but they were rare. These were the people who had unique relationships in marriage, in the office, and at home. And they also had connections with outstanding positive-thinking churches. But on an overall average, Dr. Hall said this group had 75 percent negative input.

Dr. Hall's closing comment was, "You see, Doctor Schuller, we are fighting against tremendous odds. The average human being (who is trying to be positive) is fighting a losing battle, unless he's tied into something unusual that constantly feeds him positive emotions."

Do you wonder why you don't have the *up* feeling all the time? Do you wonder why you want to quit and give up? Do you wonder why you lack enthusiasm and inner spiritual power? It's quite simple.

The majority of thoughts and inputs that come into that brain of yours—that soul of yours—is negative! That's right! That's why you need to attend a church where every service is positive. You need it! That's why we print books and try desperately to get you to do at least one positive thing every day. You need it! I need it! Everyone needs it!

How to Receive Satisfaction in Life

Recently I read about Doctor William Havender, a prominent ophthalmologist. He was addressing a group of young medical students about to graduate. He said: "Students, when I was your age I could only conclude that no one knew about God. And therefore atheism was the only tenable position. Now, I know whether or not there is a God; the patients that know they have a God are much better off than those who do not believe in God. There is no question about it. There is an enormous difference! So what do we physicians do about that fact? Let me illustrate by comparing physicians to stoneworkers.

"Three stoneworkers might, depending upon their viewpoint or their perspective or their mental attitude, look upon their job in different ways. One stoneworker sees his job as carrying stone; another stoneworker sees it as building a wall; and another sees his job as creating a cathedral to the glory of God. As doctors, you have the same attitude. If you see your job as carrying stones, you will then see your patients as complaining crocks, indigent invalids, sick scoundrels, and poor protoplasm. And with that view you will soon start seeking the solace of alcohol or drugs.

"A second attitude is you can see your work as the construction of an endless wall, the futile patching up of wornout bodies. The whole endeavor becomes senseless because you know, ultimately, that the body cannot be patched up anymore. Now with that attitude, you welcome the ultimate escape from your profession, because you'll think that at the end you're a loser and you'll welcome death.

"But if you are as fortunate as I am to come to believe that there is a God and every human being is one of His unique and special creatures, however frail and faulted they might be, then you will look upon each patient as a little cathedral—as an individual that you can build to the glory of God. I am now able to see each patient as a very special person—a child of God—deserving my best skill and attention as I rebuild that cathedral!

"What I am doing is very important, and of course, my patients sense my new attitude. They are so grateful. And any doctor is going to be happy when he is dealing with appreciative patients.

"Finally, the most important thing that I can ever say to you is: 'Live your life, doctors, as if there was a God, even if you don't believe in Him! Live your life and your practice as if there was a God of love that cares for you, too, even as He cares for every patient that comes in! And you know what? With that attitude you'll someday be an old silver-haired and wrinkle-faced doctor, but you will still have a twinkle in your eye and love in your life!' "

The Cost of Perfect Love

You have all walked past a jewelry store and looked into the window, staring at all the beautiful jewels. You may see a little ring with a price tag of fourteen dollars or a silver neck chain that is twenty dollars, or perhaps an attractive gold bracelet that is only ten dollars. Then you see a stunning piece of jewelry that catches your eye, but the price tag is turned over. You think it's probably not too expensive, so you go in and ask the clerk what it costs. He turns the price tag over and you're shocked at the cost!

The most priceless pieces of jewelry—the kind that become lasting family heirlooms—are always made out of authentic metals and jewels. They are never cheap. So perfect love has a high price tag! It's like expensive jewelry—it's not cheap. Perfect love always calls for costly commitments to care—always.

The Result of Fear

Once I attended a rather prestigious affair in Hong Kong. (Actually it was a banquet.) I was sitting next to a very important gentleman—a leading citizen of the city. The table was beautifully spread when we were seated. The fruit cup, which was the starter, was already set before us. Also, in front of us were the rolls, the butter, and the dessert (which was cake, as I remember). As soon as we sat down, we began to eat.

The gentleman to my right started by pushing aside the fruit cup and reaching for the dessert. He ate the piece of cake before the fruit cocktail! That struck me as rather peculiar so I said, "That's interesting— you ate the dessert first!" "Yes," he replied, laughing. "It's one of my eccentricities." An executive in a major international firm, this distinguished English gentleman explained, "I developed the habit as a child." "Oh?" I responded. "My folks always said, 'You can't eat dessert until you've finished your vegetables.'" "I'll tell you what happened with me," he went on. "My father always ate the dessert first. I can still remember him saying, 'There might be a fire so eat your dessert first!'"

These little fears do some funny things to people, don't they? I mean, if you let them get into your mind and under your skin, fears can make your decisions; fears can set your goals; fears can determine how you approach a problem, or run away from it. Before you realize it, you have surrendered leadership to your fears. And fears can kill you!

To Handle Your Foes: Keep on Shining!

I'm reminded of the judge who was campaigning for reelection. He had a reputation for integrity. He was a distinguished and honorable gentleman of no small charity. And his opponent was conducting a vicious, mud-smearing, unfair campaign against him.

Somebody approached the judge and said, "Do you know what your opponent is saying about you? Do you know he is criticizing you? How are you going to handle it? What are you going to do about it?'' The judge looked at his counselors and his campaign committee and calmly replied: ''Well, when I was a boy I had a dog. And every time the moon was full, that hound dog would howl and bark at the bright face of the moon. We never did sleep very well those nights. He would bark and howl at the moon all night.'' With that, the judge concluded his remarks.

''That's beside the point,'' his campaign manager impatiently said. ''You've told us a nice story about your dog, but what are you going to do about your critic?'' The judge explained. ''I just answered you! When the dog barked at the moon, the moon kept right on shining! I don't intend to do anything but keep right on shining. And I'll ignore the criticism, like the moon ignored the dog. I'll just keep right on shining! Quietly, calmly, beautifully!''

Remember that! It might give you courage to shine—to strive for the top and not worry about what people will say if you succeed or if you fail.

You May Be a Late Bloomer

A student from a wealthy family barely made it through Harrow, a very famous English undergraduate school. His family wanted him to attend a very prestigious university upon his graduation from Harrow, but the young boy had to be tutored three times by a private tutor before he could even get into the upper-level-school. ''I don't believe this child went through Harrow," the learned tutor exclaimed. "I think he went under Harrow. He's just not very bright!" That student's name was Winston Churchill!

There are lots of late bloomers, and if you've got courage, and you won't be discouraged if you come in second again and again and again. Someday you may well end up being Number One! But if you don't have courage, you will quit, and then you'll never succeed!

The Courage to Face Failure

Over fifty years ago, a little lady named Lillian married a graduate of the Princeton Theological Seminary. As a minister's wife, her name changed to Lillian Dickson. She and her young husband prayed earnestly together. "God, You have a plan for our lives. Where should we spend it? What shall we do with it?" Now, they had courage. They dared to believe that they could have the number-one slot. They were willing to take a number-two spot if that's what God wanted for them, because the Reverend Dickson said, "Remember this, Lillian, let's spend our lives where the need is greatest!" That judgment led them to an island called Formosa.

So, over fifty years ago, they sailed across the ocean to help the impoverished, the lost, the illiterate, the sick, and dying in Formosa.

When they arrived, they talked to a government official in Social Services. He looked at this young naive couple and laughed. "Look, go back to America. You can't possibly succeed here. There is no way. No way!" He stood up and walked over to the window and pointed outside. "Look out that window. You can see the ocean. You want to help people? Helping people here in Formosa is like getting one bucket of water out of that vast ocean." But young Lillian Dickson got out of her chair and said, "Well, then I am going to fill my bucket!"

That was over fifty years ago. It was just four years ago, I recall, that I was with Lillian Dickson at a banquet. At that time, her husband had died. Today she is still alive. Today she is still on that island. Fifty plus years later she is nearly eighty years of age, and she has a new ten-year plan! And what has her bucket amounted to?

Well, Lillian Dickson has established over one thousand churches, schools, and hospitals! It all happened because she was willing to fail! To face possible futility! If she and her husband hadn't had the courage to fail, they would have turned right around and gone home. They would have accomplished nothing. You see, when you think you've failed, you don't know what your bucket of water may have accomplished. God uses ordinary people who think they are failures, and they make the world go round! They really do!

The Truth About Babe Ruth

Everybody knows the name of a man who, until a few years ago, held the world's record for the most home-run hits in the major leagues. He hit 714 home runs, holding the world record, until 1976 when Hank Aaron passed him. His name was Babe Ruth. But how many people remember the name of the man who held the record for the greatest number of strikeouts? As I recall, the record book shows that this fellow had 1,330 strikeouts. That's the record. And I think it still holds. But how many people know his name? You just remember Babe Ruth who won the home-run record.

It was in 1927. The Yankees were playing in Philadelphia. That's when Babe Ruth got one of his home runs. You may have read the story. He came up to the plate for the first time. Babe missed the first pitch, strike. The second pitch, another strike. Swish, strike three! The second time he came up to bat he struck at the first one, strike one; struck at the second one, strike two; and the third one, strike three! Now it was the eighth inning and the Yankees were behind, three to one. The bases were loaded. Thirty-five thousand fans were on their feet as Babe Ruth came up to bat for the third time. Everyone knew that Lefty Grove could strike him out again.

First pitch, strike; second pitch, he swung so hard that when he missed, he stumbled and fell on the ground. He picked up his pudgy body, dusted himself off, put his cap back on, and waited for the third pitch. It was so fast, nobody even saw it. All they heard was a crack, and that ball went out of the stadium, over the roofs of the houses, across the street from the park for one of the longest hits in the major leagues. All the fellows on the bases came running in, and when Babe Ruth came across home plate, the Home-Run King took his hat off to the fans and smiled. You remember him—Babe Ruth, the Home-Run King! But how many of you remember the name of the guy who still today, holds the record for the number of strikeouts—1,330—his name, too, is Babe Ruth! Yes, Babe Ruth would never have become the Home-Run King if he had feared the failures of strikeouts!

The Malibu Rock

Here is a true story that will amaze you—a story that happened recently. It's about California and Australia. In a way, it's a story that concerns you and me.

Not far from our church is a town called Malibu, situated below high hills which overlook the waves of the Pacific Ocean, as they roll over the sandy shoreline. On one particular hill stood a massive rock— a rock that had been there for thousands upon thousands of years. Californians drove by it for decades without thinking much of it. But one day a home-owner in Malibu looked up and thought to himself, *If that rock falls, my property will be destroyed.* So he organized a citizens group, and together they prepared a class-action suit against the California Highway Department, charging it with liability in the event the rock should fall. Members of the citizens group had actually climbed up to the rock and inspected it. They were sure they had seen signs of movement.

Under the threat of a class-action suit, the highway department was forced to assume the impending liability, and so accepted the responsibility for removing what was to become known throughout the country as the "Malibu Rock." They employed two of their most powerful bulldozers to dislodge the massive rock, but even together their strength was not enough to move it. Next they used a helicopter with cables an inch thick attached to the rock in combinations with the two bulldozers. Together they strained to move the rock, but it would not budge.

Finally they employed a force so powerful that by it, through time, enormous mountains and hills have been leveled—a force that nothing could resist for long—the force of rushing water. For four days and nights water under high pressure was pumped against the rock. Then the bulldozers and helicopter once again thrust their might against the huge rock and managed to dislodge it. To everyone's surprise it was discovered that the bulk of the rock was not above ground but so far beneath the surface that chances are it would never have rolled down that hill in a million years!

Nevertheless, the job was done. The rock fell and rolled into the middle of the highway. By the time the entire operation was completed it cost California taxpayers $1 million. And, ironically, the fears of the homeowners who sought the removal of the threatening rock were realized. The rock had been holding up the whole hill. When the rock was removed, mud slid down the hill and their properties were, in fact, damaged. Although they never realized it until it was too late, that rock had been their best friend.

Meanwhile, watching the media coverage of the removal of the Malibu Rock from his hotel room in Los Angeles was a young man from Australia. This young man was a possibility thinker. He saw the rock—not as a menace—but as a masterpiece. His name is Brett Livingston Strong. When he was fifteen years old, he painted a beautiful picture of a naked aborigine gazing up at the Sydney Opera House. The work was so widely acclaimed that the Queen of England accepted it on behalf of her country. At twenty-three he came to America with hopes of furthering his career as an artist.

When he heard the rock was coming down, he rushed to the site in Malibu and saw it roll into the middle of the highway. At once, he approached members of the highway department and said, "I want to buy the rock." The highway officials poked each other and snickered. They sold the rock for one hundred dollars. The young Australian felt he had just bought the best bargain of his life, as he traded his check for the receipt.

"Oh, by the way," the highway officials said, "There's just one more thing you need to know. You've got to get that rock out of the middle of the road in the next forty-eight hours." But his enthusiasm was not dampened. He set about planning how he would remove his twenty-ton rock from the center of a California highway.

He went to Century Plaza in Los Angeles and convinced the merchants there that the rock would make a beautiful addition to their landscaping scheme. The

merchants agreed. So he collected an investment of
twenty thousand dollars, with which to have the rock
hauled to Century City. He covered the rock with a
tarpaulin and, working ten hours a day with pneu-
matic hammers, from February 1979 to May 1979, he
chiseled out of the Malibu Rock the figure of a man
who, for him, the rock epitomized. "The rock re-
minds me of John Wayne," Brett Livingston Strong
said. "Tough to bring down."

Not far from the site in Century City where Brett
was working on sculpturing the rock into the image
of John Wayne is a hospital called UCLA Medical
Center. At that time a dear friend and neighbor of
ours, named John Wayne, was a patient there. When
Brett finished his sculpture of the "Big Duke," John
Wayne left his hospital room before he died to look
at the majestic work. "I like it," he said. "I really
like it."

In Scottsdale, Arizona, a wealthy philanthropist
named Tom Murphy was impressed by the sculpture
and came to the young artist and offered to buy it.
And the story that is circulating is that the sculpture
was purchased by Mr. Murphy for $1 million. And
guess what? The latest gossip is the rock is going back
up the hill to be placed in the J. Paul Getty Museum
—only a couple of miles down the road from where it
originally stood! So some saw the rock as a risk—but
a young possibility thinker saw it as an opportunity!

There are two kinds of people in this world today
—possibility thinkers and impossibility thinkers. Impossibility thinkers are constantly looking for ways
of avoiding possible risks. They want insurance that
covers every eventuality of life. Impossibility thinkers are seeking a risk-free society. On the other hand

possibility thinkers realize there is no way to achieve success without being a sanctified risk taker.

Viktor Frankl's Stars

Viktor Frankl, an eminent Jewish psychiatrist, was standing naked and stripped before the Gestapo. They had taken his watch, then had seen his gold wedding band, and demanded it as well. As Frankl took the wedding band off his finger to hand it to the Gestapo officer, a thought went through his brain. *There is one thing you can never take from me and that is my freedom to choose how I will react to whatever you do to me!* That we all retain to the end.

If you choose to react positively, not negatively, to the hurts of life, you can turn your scars into stars.

Nobody Has a Money Problem, Only Idea Problems

The greatest compliment I think I've ever received came from a black cabdriver in New York City. I came out of my hotel and walked up to the first of several cabs lined against the curb. The driver was a black man with a gold ring in his nose. Immediately I experienced some cross-cultural conflict—he scared me! But before I could say hello, the man jumped out of the cab, pointed a finger at me and shouted, " 'Hour of Power'! You're Doctor Robert Schuller, aren't you?" Then he shook my hand, embraced me, and opened the door. I slid in, and he told me how our ministry has changed his life.

He was born in Harlem, and the man never knew his father. All his life he lived on welfare. He tuned into the "Hour of Power" one day and became a regular viewer.

"Doctor Schuller, me and my wife watched you," he said. "We liked to see the flowers, oranges, and palm trees—especially in the winter. It was just nice to look at. When you started talking about possibility thinking, I thought, *Yeah, you can talk that way. You're white. You live in California. Anybody who lives by Disneyland can believe in possibility thinking!*

"But then you told a story that changed my life. It was about some negative-thinking women who lived on the bayou in Louisiana, who were constantly complaining about their homes and lives. Finally one positive-thinking woman got tired of their complaining and said to them, 'Look, you live on the bayou. The bayou flows into the river. The river flows into the Gulf. The Gulf flows into the ocean. You have a boat. You can go anywhere from where you are!' "

So the man began to wonder if possibility thinking could work for him. "Why don't you get a job?" his wife suggested. "What can I do?" he demanded defensively. "You can drive," she retorted. "Why don't you become a cabdriver?" "If they knew I was black, they would never hire me," he countered. "That's impossibility thinking—just what Doctor

Schuller preaches against," she persisted. So finally the man was persuaded. He went to the telephone and called the cab company. When he told them he wanted a job, they asked him, "Are you black?" "Yes, I am, " he responded defensively, his heart sinking. "Great!" they said, "We need black cab-drivers. The whites don't dare drive in Harlem. You come in and you've got a job!"

As he told the story, his eyes filled with tears. He had such pride in himself and his work. "I earn more now as a cabdriver than I ever did on welfare!" he enthused. He has the pride of being a wage earner.

It's very easy to be negative. It's very easy to say, "Poor me. See what I don't have?" We all need more. But do you know what we need more of? Not a handout—but dynamic ideas to turn us into produc-tive persons.

How to Face Your Future

The other day I came home and saw my youngest daughter, Gretchen, sitting on the floor in her room. Scattered all over the carpet in front of her were en-velopes and sheets of clean, unwrinkled stationery. With pen in hand it looked like she was getting ready to write some letters. Now, I know that Gretchen never writes letters, so my curiosity was instantly stirred.

"Gretchen," I exclaimed, "what are you doing?" Caught by surprise, she turned and looked up at me. "Oh, hi, Dad. I'm going to write my thank-you notes." "You're what?" I asked. "What do you mean?" "I'm starting to write my thank-you notes for my Christmas gifts," she explained. A little confused at this point, I went on. "Gretchen, how in the world can you write thank-you notes for gifts that you haven't received yet? How do you know who to address them to? And how do you know that you'll be receiving any?" "Oh," she enthused, "I've got that figured out. I'm going to say, 'Dear Friend, Thank you for your wonderful gift. I'm enjoying it very much. Love, Gretchen.' " I laughed and said, "But, Gretchen, how do you know you are going to enjoy all the gifts?" "Oh, Daddy, I just know I'm going to enjoy every one of them!" That's what you call advance planning! She was in such good spirits, because she was expecting something beautiful to happen. She was already living in her imagination in the arena of goodness.

Some people spend most of their lives living in the past arena of bad news. Something that happened to you yesterday is past! Expect good things to happen to you today and live high! Live in the realm of good news! Don't live in the realm of bad news!

There's Something Good in Every Situation

A young man named Woolworth decided he was going to open a new store—a brand-new business of his own. When he was ready for the grand opening, a merchant down the street got a little nervous about this young man taking some of his business away, so he ran an ad in the local paper. It read: DO YOUR

LOCAL SHOPPING HERE. WE HAVE BEEN IN BUSINESS
FOR FIFTY YEARS! Young Woolworth couldn't believe it! How could he handle this competition? What
should he do? The next week he countered with an ad
of his own. And it read: WE'VE BEEN IN BUSINESS
ONLY ONE WEEK—ALL OF OUR MERCHANDISE IS
BRAND-NEW! And he was off to a great success!

Take all the good news you can. If you're faced
with bad news, remember, oftentimes there is good
news hidden in a bad-news scene. You have to become positively oriented before you see it.

Take All the Good News
You Can Get

On my way into church early last Sunday morning
somebody called out my name. "Doctor Schuller!" I
stopped and turned around. A young man was trying
to get my attention. "I wanted to catch you before
you went into your office," the man said. "Do you
remember a little boy named Nelson—you prayed for
him two years ago?" I couldn't recall, until he gave
me some of the background on the child, and then I
remembered. A car had suddenly gone out of control
and through a backyard fence, pinning this five-
year-old boy under the car. He was rushed to the
hospital with a badly crushed neck. Doctors gave him
little chance to live. The father of the boy saw the
huge cross on the top of the Tower of Hope and came
to our church for help. He knelt by the Good
Shepherd statue, crying and praying that his son

would live. One of the ministers found him and counseled him, trying to comfort him during this time.

After talking with the minister, the father realized that this was the church that was on television each Sunday morning. He then requested that I go see his boy. I'll never forget that child—tiny, naked, and barely breathing—lying in the crib. An iron skull, like a cross of thorns, made out of steel, penetrated into his tiny skull, pulling his head out. Iron clamps were on his tiny feet stretching his tiny, frail body. He lay there motionless, pale, and quiet, on the edge of eternity.

I prayed and prayed for little Nelson, but I never knew what happened to the little boy after that day. And then this young man came up to me with some great news. He said, "Doctor Schuller, that little boy is the child of some very good friends of mine. My wife and I were in their home this week, and that little boy has completely recovered!" Taken back by the good news, I said, "But he had a broken neck. You mean he isn't paralyzed?" "No," the young man said. "The bones were so crushed that there wasn't a bone of substantial size to sever a nerve. The nerves were never cut! He's perfectly normal in every way!"

What good news to greet me at the beginning of a new day! Take all the good news you can! Look for it; you can spot it! And try to develop a callousness for the bad news. If there's bad news, turn it into good news through possibility thinking. Take all the good news that you can!

Break All the Good News You Can

Never will I forget the time that I was invited to make a call on Hubert Humphrey. This was after he told me that he had an inoperable cancer and that he would not return to Washington ever again. I called on him in his Minneapolis apartment. His close friends approached me before I knocked on the door. "Doctor Schuller, if you could just inspire him to return to Washington, we would be forever grateful. We think his last days would be more meaningful there. We don't know how long those days, months, or years will be."

As I stepped into his apartment, I saw a gaunt and lean man who after having an ileostomy, colostomy, chemotherapy, and radiation treatment, had changed drastically. But there was still a sparkle in his eye, as he greeted me and welcomed me to Minneapolis, Minnesota.

I was a little nervous about what to talk about, but once we got started it was easy. We talked about his prognosis. Then we began to thank God for all He'd done—for the successful surgeries that my friend had gone through; for his beautiful wife, Muriel; for his lovely daughter and her little mongoloid child, who has brought so much joy into Hubert's and Muriel's lives; for the many years of service to his country; for the excellent medical care; that there is always hope even though everything may seem hopeless; that when it seems nothing can happen for good, suddenly there can be a total turnabout and we see the light; for Jesus Christ who came to the world to give us courage in tough times and hope in dark times and an awareness that what seems like the end of the road is only a bend in the road of life. Instead of dwelling on the negative, we concentrated on the positive. And we had a beautiful time together, sharing good news!

"God Loves You, and I'm Trying"

It was Christmas Eve, and I was running late, so my wife and two girls jumped into the car and we took off for church, trying to make the service on time. As we neared the campus of the church, I suddenly realized that I had to make a left turn. I was in the right lane, so I hurriedly looked into my rearview mirror, saw that nobody was behind me, and swerved over into the left lane. Well, what I didn't see was a guy in my blind spot! I cut him off and almost clipped his front bumper. I don't normally drive that way; I try to be very careful, but I just didn't see him behind me. I made the lane, just as the light turned red.

Well, the next thing I knew, a large man was standing outside my car, motioning me to roll down my window. He was furious! I could see the blood vessels swelling in his neck! And his mouth was expelling some words I can't repeat. Hesitating a moment, I rolled down my window and tried to say I was sorry. But he wouldn't let me utter a word! I have never heard so many obscenities in my life. I tried to interrupt him, but he would just go off on another tangent. I tried to smile but that even made him madder. Finally, he had to take a breath and I moved in.

"Hey! Wait a minute! You know what? It's Christmastime . . . ." But he had taken a deep breath and started in again. I wanted to break some good news, but he wouldn't give me the chance. Fortunately, he had to take another breath, so I jumped in again. (Now I know why God made the lungs with a limited capacity—it's the only way negative people can be turned off for a second.) I looked him in the eye and I said, "God loves you, and I'm trying!" And I saw a look come across his face that I've seen many times when people recognize me in a restaurant or an airport. He got a little pink in the face and went back to his car without saying another word.

Break all the good news you can! You can do this by sharing your faith! Good news doesn't just happen. *You* make it happen!

"What a Pitcher!"

I am reminded of the story of the little boy overheard talking to himself as he strutted through the backyard, baseball cap in place, toting ball and bat. "I'm the greatest baseball player in the world," he said proudly. Then he tossed the ball into the air, swung at it—and missed. Undaunted, he picked up the ball, threw it into the air and, as he said to himself, "I'm the greatest ball player ever!" he swung at the ball again. And again he missed. He paused a moment to carefully examine his bat and ball. Then once again he threw the ball into the air. "I'm the greatest baseball player who ever lived!" he said. He swung the bat hard and again, he missed the ball.

"Wow!" he exclaimed. "What a pitcher!"

There's nothing in the world like a positive mental attitude. It can transform situations and experiences in life into great possibilities.

The Sky Is Falling

Not too long ago America warned the world that Sky Lab was going to fall to earth. I have a friend who was in Australia during that time. He made some very interesting observations. "Everywhere I went in Australia people were talking about the probability of Sky Lab falling into the country. Inevitably they reacted in two totally different ways. Some people reacted fearfully. 'Oh,' they exclaimed, 'what if it hits our property?' They saw Sky Lab's imminent descent to earth as a potential menace. Others reacted not with a negative, but with a positive mental attitude. 'What if it lands on our place?' they said. 'Won't it be a valuable souvenir? We could even take it to San Francisco and collect the ten thousand dollars cash reward offered by the San Francisco newspaper.' "

When Sky Lab did fall to earth, it did, in fact, fall in Australia. Some of the people on whose property it fell never touched it for fear of contracting radioactive poisoning. But one young man believed what he had been told about the pieces of Sky Lab being absolutely safe to touch. He flew to San Francisco with his piece of Sky Lab and collected the ten thousand dollars in cash. Because he held onto a positive attitude, Sky Lab was no menace to him; it was a masterpiece!

A natural law states that whenever a person begins to practice a positive mental attitude, there is a power released—a very natural, human power. God designed human beings so that we produce constructive energy when we think positively and begin to sense the unlimited possibilities in little ideas.

Knott's Berry Farm

I have a dear friend named Walter Knott. Some of you may have visited Knott's Berry Farm in Southern California. It is one of the first comprehensive recreational parks to be founded in America—a favorite place visited by tourists from all over the world.

Walter Knott and his wife, Cornelia, started their now-famous enterprise only a few miles from our church. They began many years ago by raising boysenberries. Today it's hard to believe how much mileage they've gotten out of a boysenberry!

A few years ago Walter Knott stood in the pulpit of this church. "What gives you your greatest fulfillment, Walter?" I asked him. "My greatest fulfillment comes from the knowledge that I am creating job opportunities for hundreds of people," he answered. "It takes me only five thousand dollars of capital investment to create one new job," he calculated. Of course that was a few years ago. But as a successful capitalist, Walter Knott saw his situation as an opportunity to create job opportunities for people. Isn't that beautiful! One small idea has such tremendous reproductive capacity!

Melrose Suspension Bridge

In California we are very proud of the beautiful San Francisco Golden Gate Bridge. As a suspension bridge, it is an architectural marvel, still unsurpassed in beauty and grace. However such a feat of engineering followed a history of suspension bridges, and one cannot ignore the influence of the Melrose Suspension Bridge, which spans the Niagara River.

In 1848 an engineer by the name of Theodore Elliot solved a problem that had hindered commerce for decades. For years farmers and businessmen alike had thought how wonderful it would be to have a railroad that could cross from New York to Canada. But in order to build such a railroad, a bridge was needed to span the Niagara River. Traditional bridge-building schemes simply would not work. But Theodore Elliot conceived of a brilliant solution. He proposed the first suspension bridge. He envisioned supportive towers twenty-four and eighty feet high on either side of the roaring, raging waters of the Niagara River. From the towers he would suspend a cable which in turn would support the bridge.

But he had one problem. How could he get started? There was no way to work from a boat at that point on the river. There was no shoreline to work from, only sheer, rocky cliffs. And yet he knew that beginning was half-done.

So he decided to start by stringing a cable from one side of the river to the other. "A cable made from thirty-six strands of number ten wire will be thick and sturdy enough to suspend two buckets capable of holding two workers. These workers could go from side to side and begin construction of the bridge," he said. "But how can you get a steel cable that thick across the gorge?" someone asked. "You can't throw it across. It's too heavy." Elliot was puzzled for a moment. Then he got an idea: Why not have a contest for the kids in the neighborhood—a kite-flying contest?

Elliot announced the kite-flying contest and offered a prize of ten dollars to the first boy who could fly a kite across the gorge and tie the rope down on the other side. There were many contestants—ten dollars was a lot of money for a little lad in those days. But none succeeded, until one day an eleven-year-old boy named Homer Walsh took advantage of a good south wind. His kite took off and, instead of falling short as all the others had, it landed on the other side. His friend, who was waiting across the river, tied the string down on the other side. Homer won the ten dollars!

The next day Elliot tied the kite string to a slightly heavier rope. He pulled the rope across the gorge, so that it spanned the gap. Then he tied that rope to still-thicker rope and pulled it across. This rope he attached to the steel cable and, by repeating the process, he strung the cable from one side of the gorge to the other, thus enabling the two workers to move back and forth and begin the construction of the suspension bridge.

You may be faced with what seems to be a risky but insignificant decision. It may be only a kite string, but like Homer's kite string, it can pave the way for something as monumental as the first suspension bridge. Just like Theodore Elliot and Homer Walsh, you may be the inspiration for great future accomplishments—as great as the Golden Gate Bridge! Next time you pass over the Golden Gate say a word of thanks to a little boy named Homer Walsh.

What Makes a Large Fish?

Some of you know that as a hobby I raise Japanese carp known as koi fish. These fish are really amazing creatures. Some of the larger ones will actually suck my fingers (they have no teeth), and let me stroke them on the back.

The carp are used to taking a whole slice of bread and passing it around to one another, taking a bite as they do. One day I was leaning over the pool and my wallet fell into the water. I watched as one fish passed it to another, hoping they would soon tire of the game. (I called it carp-to-carp walleting.)

Some people have asked, "Why are there some big fish and some little ones? How big can they get?" That's a fascinating question. The size of the fish depends on the size of the pond. A koi fish can live in a small tank, but it will never grow longer than two or three inches. In a larger pond they can grow from six to ten inches. In ponds the size of mine, they will grow up to a foot and a half in length. But if they live in a huge lake where they can swim and stretch, they will grow up to three feet long. It's the stretching that lends itself to greater growth. The size of the fish is in direct relation to the size of the pond.

This observation leads to an interesting principle: Little ideas which fall into little-thinking minds produce little achievements. But when those same little ideas drop into big-thinking minds, they become enormous achievements! The size of your thinking determines the growth of your idea in its ultimate development!

Fence Out

Not long ago I read a story about a salesman who, in 1800, came from the East to a small frontier town in Texas. He came to sell his goods to the merchant at the local general store. Just as the salesman was about to show the storekeeper his merchandise, a local rancher came in to make a purchase.

"Excuse me," the merchant said, "but I have to wait on my customer." Turning to the rancher he said, "What can I do for you, Josh?" Josh pointed to several items around the store, and then asked the storekeeper to put the things on his account.

"Oh," the storekeeper said knowingly, "so you want credit. Let me ask you something, Josh. Are you doing any fencing this spring?" "Yes, I am, sir," Josh replied. "Well, are you fencing in or are you fencing out?" the merchant queried. "I'm fencing out," Josh answered. "Going to add three hundred and sixty new acres." "Well, then," the shop owner said, "if you're fencing out, go ahead and see Harry at the back of the store. He'll help you get what you need."

Having listened to this exchange, the salesman was somewhat puzzled. "You know," he said, "I've heard of all kinds of systems of credit, but I've never heard of your system. What kind of credit is that?"

"Well," the merchant explained, "we've got two kinds of ranchers and farmers here—those who fence in and those who fence out. Those who fence in are people who are afraid they might not make it quite as well next year. They are afraid of what the weather might bring, or of wasting too much seed, so they pull their fences in. Then there are others who have confidence in themselves and their work. Slowly, gradually, they fence out, adding a little more land to their farms and ranches. People who fence out have hope. And I give credit to anyone who has hope!"

Life's Greatest Prizes

After several months in our first drive-in church, we were finally able to afford our first professional minister of music. Her name was Lea Ora Mead, and she took charge of our first choir (composed of an odd number of volunteer singers who met for rehearsals in our home). When we first hired Lea Ora, I took her aside and said, "Lea Ora, we don't want to build just an average church. We want to do something that's really outstanding, and so we want our music to be outstanding. With God's help, I know you can lay the musical foundations, so that this church will have the finest quality music heard anywhere. If the foundations are laid correctly, we know the rest will fall into place."

Lea Ora did that. For six years we conducted this church in the drive-in theater. Every Sunday morning I climbed up on the sticky tar-paper roof of the snack bar and delivered my messages in the rain, the chilly wind, or the blazing sun. And standing right behind me, leading the choir, was Lea Ora Mead. When we finally moved into a building of our own, she continued to direct the choir and bring beautiful music into the lives of countless people.

Lea Ora is still a young woman, but today she is dying of cancer. She has been fighting it courageously for a long time; and we don't know how many more days she has left to go on fighting.

Recently, someone who prefers to remain anonymous sent the first gift for the Pillars of Steel in the Crystal Cathedral in Lea Ora's honor. So Lea Ora became our first "Iron-Pillared Friend."

I went to call on Lea Ora one night. She had received the medallion and a letter informing her of the gift given in her name. When we greeted one another, she was crying. "Bob, who gave that gift for me?" she asked. "Lea Ora," I explained gently, "the giver of the gift asked to remain anonymous." "Yes," she continued, "But who would do something like that? I moved away from here years ago. Who could possibly remember me?" Taking her hand in mine, I looked at her and replied, "Lea Ora, stop and think of every person who ever heard music while you were choir director of our church. Think of all the people who might have been inspired and lifted because of your ministry. You brought a lot of joy into a lot of people's lives."

There's no way she could ever guess who it was who chose to commemorate her contribution to the church. As I turned to leave, she said, "You know, maybe I really did something worthwhile in my life after all." "Lea Ora," I assured her, "there's no way you can ever know how much good you did for people in your lifetime, for music has a way of reaching into the hidden corners of the mind and heart and stirring a soul."

As I've said before, any fool can count the seeds in an apple, but only God can count the apples in a seed. When you draw near to the end of your life and you feel that you've done something wonderful for God—that you've been an inspiration to a fellow human being—then you have received one of life's greatest prizes.

Jim Poppen

Jim Poppen was a student at Hope Academy, a high-school division of my alma mater, Hope College. But Jim was not exactly an exemplary student. There were people at that institution who questioned his intellectual capacity. Many of his teachers remarked, "I don't think he is ever going to amount to much. Jim Poppen just isn't very bright."

But to prejudge the intellect of another is one of the most audacious presumptions anyone can be guilty of. We know that child prodigies are not born;

they are developed. That scientifically proven statement was first introduced to me in Paris at the International Psychological Conference. If a child prodigy is developed and not born, then the average person has the potential for becoming a genius.

Jim Poppen graduated from Hope Academy and astounded his former teachers by going on to study at Northwestern University.

One Christmas, Jim's father awoke suddenly when he heard a noise in the night. Convinced that there was a burglar in the house, Mr. Poppen stole downstairs and tiptoed into the dark kitchen. There he found Jim tying knots around chair legs as fast as he could. Sure that his son had flipped, Mr. Poppen exclaimed, "Jim, what in the world are you doing?" "It's okay, Dad," Jim explained. "I've decided I'm going to be a brain surgeon. I've got to teach my fingers to tie knots very fast and accurately where I cannot see anything—just like a surgeon operating on a human skull."

His father laughed that night, but Jim did become a brain surgeon—one of the best in the world. When Bobby Kennedy was shot at the Biltmore Hotel in Los Angeles, Dr. Jim Poppen was chosen by the President of the United States to fly to Bobby Kennedy's side and attempt to save his life.

William Loeb, from New Hampshire, a listener to "Hour of Power," recently sent me an editorial from his newspaper the *Manchester Union Leader*, about Jim Poppen. The letter says, "Doctor Schuller, you mentioned Jim Poppen as a friend of yours. He was my friend too. Did you know he died just a few months ago? I think you should know a little more about him.

"You have spoken of Dr. Poppen's connection with Bobby Kennedy and the attempt on his life. Did you know that just a few months before that tragic incident Aristotle Onassis' only son was involved in an airplane crash? Jim Poppen, accompanied by Aristotle and his wife, Jackie Kennedy Onassis, sped across the Atlantic in a Lear jet to Greece to be by the young man's side. International leaders, ministers of finance, presidents, and kings knew Jim Poppen as the greatest brain surgeon in the world.

"Just a year ago," the letter continued, "I wanted to reach Doctor Poppen. By telephone, I finally tracked him down in a remote village 12,000 feet high in the Andes, in Bogota, Colombia. 'What in the world are you doing in Bogota, Jim?' I asked incredulously. 'Oh,' he replied very quietly and matter-of-factly, 'There are some people here who have some problems. They can't afford the high cost of medical care in Boston, so I decided to come here and take care of them.'

"When Jim Poppen died a few months ago, the services held for him in the New England Baptist Memorial Chapel were jammed with great people, whose famous faces many would know. But there were also many unknowns present—red, yellow, black, white, rich and poor. Many nurses came to the chapel directly from the operating rooms. They stood quietly in the back of the chapel, still dressed in their green surgical robes and caps. Hundreds came to pay tribute to a man who proved that, by giving life all you've got, you can leave a mark behind and do something beautiful."

God has a prize for you. If you will trust Him with your life, you will have the incomparably beautiful assurance that you have done something great for God.

There Is Hope for All of Us

Here's another story about this very remarkable human being, Jim Poppen. This amazing man used to hunt ferocious jaguars in the jungles of Brazil, using a .22 short bullet. Once, when he told a fellow hunter what kind of ammunition he preferred, the hunter asked derisively, "Why don't you just use a slingshot?" "But a twenty-two short is plenty good for hunting a jaguar," he argued. "After all, I aim at the eye." When asked how he expected to hit the eye of a jaguar he replied, "Simple. I just close in to thirty or forty feet."

Of course, anyone who hunts knows that a Brazilian jaguar can jump forty to sixty feet easily. "They're not going to jump," he explained, "because I stand at the end of the branch the jaguar is standing on and swing it back and forth to keep it off balance. It can't possibly jump!" He was an incredible man!

God's Unconditional Love

We have some very dear friends who live on a farm in Minnesota. God blessed them with two sons, but their first son died in a tragic drowning accident when he was a teenager. The couple was heart-broken, but they comforted themselves with this thought: *We still have a beautiful son. We still have a wonderful marriage. We'll look at what we have left, not at what we've lost.* But two years later their remaining son was killed in a farm accident, when his tractor rolled over on him and crushed him.

Not long after that second sad event, the couple came to visit us here at Garden Grove Community Church. "How did you pick up the pieces of your life and keep on going?" I asked them. "We received letter from across the country," the woman replied. "One letter, which was from someone we had never met, was especially comforting. It simply said, 'After what's happened, we just want to tell you that God still loves you. Nothing can stop that.' "

One of the most beautiful rewards of salvation is the awareness of God's unconditional, undying, imperishable love. No matter what happens, He has a plan of infinite beauty for your life.

He Loves Me

Yesterday our youngest daughter, Gretchen, and I were out in the garden cutting fresh flowers. Rather mischievously, I clipped one and said to her, "Gretchen, this one is for you." Then as I pulled off the petals one by one, I recited a rhyme from my youth: "She loves me. She loves me not. She loves me. . . ." Gretchen got a quizzical kind of expression on her face and said, "I know, Daddy. I'm going to pick one for God." And as she plucked the petals of the flower, she gave me a lesson I'll not soon forget. As she pulled the first petal, she said, "He loves me." Then she pulled the next, "He loves me." And the next, "He loves me." Until she had but one petal left and, smiling brightly, she finished the rhyme: "He loves me."

Does God Care?

The other day I heard a story about a salesman who came home from the office to find his house in complete disarray. His wife was usually a wonderful housekeeper, so he simply couldn't understand why everything was in such a mess. "What happened?" he asked in amazement. "Remember how you always ask, 'What could you possibly be doing all day?' " his wife replied. "Well, today I didn't do it!"

If we experience troubled times because God is trying to preach to us, that is fantastic! We can always stand a good word from our ultimate Source of wisdom, can't we?

The Way in Which God Uses Troubled Times

There was once a company that required 100 percent cooperation and agreement by all the employees before they could sign up for a new pension-insurance plan. Everyone in the entire company was anxious to enter into the new plan, except for one stubborn, selfish, ego-involved man, who refused to see the benefits of the new plan. He found all kinds of reasons for not joining with the others and refused to sign the consent form. Every one of his fellow employees tried to induce him to sign, but he stubbornly refused.

Finally, his boss called him into the office. He handed the man a pen and said, "Look. Here's the paper. Here's the pen. Sign it or you're fired." Smiling cheerfully, the man picked up the pen and signed his name to the consent form. In exasperation, the man's boss demanded, "Why haven't you signed it before?" "Well," the man replied, "no one ever explained it to me so clearly before."

Often troubled times are God's way of giving us the shove we need. Sometimes we postpone a decision until He really presses us.

How to Handle Boredom

The great Christian industrialist, Foster McGaw, who is the founder of American Hospital Supply Corporation, once told me an interesting story about his father. Foster's father served as a Presbyterian pastor and missionary in Warsaw, Poland, for the greater part of his life. At the age of eighty-one he retired and returned to the United States. But Mr. McGaw found retirement dull and soon became bored. He began thinking of things he had dreamed of, but never had a chance to do.

You know, he thought to himself, *one thing I've*

*always wanted to do since I was a young man was to
become a missionary to Africa. Well, why not?*

So Mr. McGaw called his son, Foster, who was age
forty-two, the founding chairman of a multimillion dollar corporation. "Foster, this is Dad," Mr.
McGaw began. "I'm going to Africa to be a missionary. I'm going to fly to New York and make a reser-
vation on a ship to Africa. I know God will provide
the money for my ticket. All I'm saying is, I want you
to come and see me off."

Foster recalls the day when his father set sail. "Of
course I was the way God provided for my father's
ticket. I still remember my last sight of him as he
stood ramrod straight, chin out, waving at me from
the upper deck. 'See ya, Foster,' he cried out. He
sailed to Africa and worked as a missionary from the
age of eighty-two to eighty-six. He died and was
buried there." Your troubled times may come when
you're old, bored, and feel nobody needs you. Let
God prod you! Let Him show you how to be produc-
tive at any age.

God Wants to Promote You

Maybe God is trying to promote you through your
troubled times. I remember counseling a member of
this church who was feeling hurt and betrayed. He
was a high-ranking executive in a major corporation.
Suddenly, for no apparent reason, he received his
dismissal notice—he was fired after seventeen years
with the company! He was unemployed for several
months. Each time he applied for a new position, the

interviewer would say, "Sorry, you're overqualified." But finally he did get a job. It is the best job he's ever had. He started at 33 percent more money per year than what he was paid in his former position; and he faces more challenge and opportunity than ever before! His dismissal was God's way of promoting him!

God Will Give You What You Need

This week I served communion to Corrie ten Boom. As some of you may know, Corrie is now over eighty years of age. By some miracle, she survived a concentration camp in Germany during World War II. She lost both her father and her sister while a prisoner. She told me a story from her childhood in Holland. One day she said to her father, "Papa, I don't think I have the faith to handle real trouble. I don't know what I'd do if you should die. I don't think I have the faith that some people have to face trouble."

Corrie's father looked at her tenderly and said, "Corrie, dear, when your father says he will send you to the store tomorrow, does he give the money to you today? No. He gives it to you when you are ready to go to the store. And if you are going on a train trip and you need money for a ticket, does your father give you the money when we decide you may take the trip? No. He gives it to you when you are at the depot, ready to buy your ticket. Corrie, God treats us the same way. He doesn't give you the faith until you need it. But when you do need it, He will certainly give it to you." Corrie's life is a testimony to the truth of that statement.

The Key to Economic Security

Today, everybody seems to have their own ideas on how to make the dollar stretch. I heard a story recently about a woman who had a very unique answer to the problem of economic security. At her funeral, the mourners were told that during her lifetime she had four husbands, and apparently she had planned all four. First, she married a millionaire. Then she married a Hollywood producer. Third, she married a life-insurance salesman. And, finally, her last husband was a mortician. Her plan worked well—*one for the money; two for the show; three to get ready; and four to go!*

If you want to achieve financial security, you don't have to marry a millionaire. I've got a better idea for you. The idea is simply this: Pray that God will give you the health, strength, and opportunity to earn some money. Then, once you've earned this money—however small that first check is—take 10 percent of it and drop it into the offering plate of your church.

Praise the Lord

I like to tell my old story of the minister with the unusual horse. This horse didn't respond to the usual commands of *whoa* and *giddy-up*. Instead, when the preacher wanted the horse to go, he would yell, "Praise the Lord!" The horse would hear this command and gallop full speed. When the preacher wanted the horse to stop, he yelled, "Amen!" When the horse heard this word, he would dig his hoofs into the dirt, sending the sand flying in a spray behind him as he came to a screeching halt.

When the preacher sold his horse to a man who was not well acquainted with religion, he told the man about the special commands he must use with the horse. "If you want the horse to go, say, 'Praise the Lord!' If you want the horse to stop, say, 'Amen.' "

The man bought the horse and set out on rocky terrain. As he approached a steep cliff, he wondered what the word for stopping was. "Praise the Lord!" He shouted. And the horse took off at a gallop. Then, just as he was about to plunge over the edge of the cliff, he remembered to shout "Amen!" And the horse dug his hoofs into the dust inches before reaching the edge of the cliff. Shaken, and very grateful, the man looked toward heaven and said, "Praise the Lord."

Praising the Lord really gives us go-power. Thank God for ideas that give you go-ahead, climb-up-the-ladder power. Then thank God that you have life.

You Are the Energy

A while back I bought an interesting flashlight. Before I decided to buy it, I asked, "How long will the battery last?" "As long as you do," the saleslady replied. "What do you mean?" I queried. "*You* are the battery," she explained. "There is no battery inside. You have to pump to make it light." I tried it, and sure enough, when I pumped the handle at the bottom of the flashlight, I generated the electricity to make the light! As soon as I stopped pumping, the light went out.

There is a beautiful principle illustrated in this little anecdote. If you make the right commitments to an idea that is beautiful, but seems impossible, all you have to do is pray and possibilitize—keep pumping! Bright ideas will come your way—ideas that come from God.

The Importance of Beauty

The importance of beauty in our lives was first impressed upon me when we hired the architect years ago to build the Tower of Hope and our sanctuary. At the time we decided to build the new structures, Richard Neutra's face had just appeared on the cover of *Time* magazine. He was recognized as one of the great architects of the twentieth century. We retained him to design the sanctuary and Tower of Hope.

When we began to explore the possible styles of architecture which would suit the purposes of our church, I said to him, "Richard, I'd like a church which incorporates the mood of the Twenty-third Psalm. 'Cool waters and green pastures' are universal tranquilizing elements." He loved the idea. "We'll do it!" he enthused. And so the structures were erected.

When we originally conceived of the plans of our present buildings, one person saw the plans and urged me to replace the grass, flowers, and pools of water with concrete. "Schuller," he exclaimed, "look at the waste of money you propose! You certainly can't eat it!" "You're wrong," I corrected, "we will eat it. We will feed emotionally on the beauty of the trees, flowers, grass, water, and sunshine. And as we sense the beauty of it all, something beautiful will happen in our lives. *Beauty isn't a luxury; it's a necessity.*"

A Letter of Sanity

Leslie Hale, an evangelist from Belfast, Ireland, told an interesting story. He was speaking in a large public meeting, when a man shouted above the heads of those gathered, "Leslie, I have to talk to you after the meeting." Leslie spoke soothing words to calm the man and assured him he would see him at the close of the meeting. When the meeting ended, again the man shouted, "Leslie Hale, I'd like to see you before this meeting is over." "The meeting is over," Leslie answered, "come see me."

The man urgently pushed his way through the crowds and reached into his pocket to withdraw a letter, which he handed to Leslie. Leslie was aware of the need for caution. In war-torn Ireland, trusting is a difficult thing. Anything, including a plastic explosive, could have been in the envelope. He didn't know what he was in for.

But when he opened the letter, he recognized the letterhead of a mental hospital. The letter was signed by the superintendent of the hospital. It read: "To whom it may concern: This is to certify that [the name of the man who delivered the letter] has been a patient at the mental hospital in Belfast, North Ireland. It is the judgment of those in authority here that he is now deemed capable of living life normally on the outside. In our judgment he is considered sane and sensible."

"Did you read it?" the man demanded. "I read it, every word," Leslie assured him. "That proves I'm sane, doesn't it?" the man implored with true desperation. "That proves I'm not crazy!" "That's right," Leslie agreed. "They should know. They're experts." "They're experts. They should know," the man repeated, smiling.

That was the only boost he needed. He returned the letter and envelope to his pocket. "I watched him go out of the door and climb on his bicycle," Leslie said. "Just before he pedaled away, he turned, smiled and said, 'Hey, let me see *your* letter.' "

Do you have a letter? I don't. Every human being, at some point in his or her life goes through an experience that involves such emotional turmoil that he or she asks, *Am I going crazy? Am I losing my mind?* It can be a horrible, frightening experience, but if you have encountered it, join the human race. It's normal. We all need the affirmation of our basic sanity once in a while.

The Comedian Without
a Voice Box

Good clean comedians are ministers of God. I remember my boss from the only other job I ever had as a young man in Chicago, Illinois. His name was Bill Bruin. Bill had had cancer of the throat which necessitated the removal of his larynx. The only way he was able to communicate was with the aid of a little instrument, three inches long, which looked like a flashlight. He would put the instrument up to his throat, and when he talked, his voice sounded like that of a robot.

But Bill turned his problem into an opportunity through possibility thinking. He developed a marvelous comedy routine. Every time there was a party, Bill became the center of attention. Just as the gathering would get kind of loud, he would make a sirenlike sound. Everybody would drop what they were doing and look around for the cops; Bill would have a laugh. He was a beautiful person—the comedian without a voice box. A beautiful person is an *amusing* person.

Take Time to Listen

Take the time to listen to people who need advice and comfort. Everybody needs a counselor at some time in their lives. I know a minister who decided to become a bartender. After years away at college and seminary, he went to school to learn how to mix drinks. He decided that most people who have problems don't talk to ministers, psychiatrists, or professional counselors. He discovered that many of the people with hurts often try to escape through alcohol at the neighborhood bar. He decided he'd have to get close to them, so for three years he worked as a bartender. He became a beautiful influence upon the lives of many people. He uplifted, guided, and taught the people who came to him for advice. And he led many to Christ and the Church.

Father of the Bride

I'll never forget when, for the first time in my life, I was the father of the bride. What a joyous event!

I must tell you I was a little worried because, at times, I can get very sentimental. I have been officiating in marriages for thirty-one years—since my ordination in 1950. At many of the weddings I've performed I have been so moved that I nearly choked up. So when I enjoyed the privilege of joining the first of my beloved daughters in marriage to a very special young man, I was afraid I would puddle up and weep with joy and happiness.

Several months before my doctor had given me some mild medication that would help keep my emotions under control. Frankly, I just threw the pills away and decided I would try possibility thinking instead. Through possibility thinking I have discovered a cure to that tearful ailment that has blighted the fathers of brides for centuries! If you're going to be the father of the bride and you're nearly overpowered by the joy and delight of the occasion, all you need to control the joy that would cause you to weep with happiness is this reminder: "Remember, Daddy, you're paying the bill." That should balance your joy for a moment.

Sheila's wedding was just naturally the kind of family event that could fill me to overflowing with happiness and love. Our three younger daughters were Sheila's bridesmaids. I was so very proud of my fourteen-year-old daughter, Carol, who so beautifully achieved the goal she had set for herself after the accident (which necessitated the amputation of her left leg). Just as she said she would, she walked down the aisle at her sister's wedding, her bouquet firmly taped to the top of her crutch.

After I had escorted my lovely daughter down the aisle and given her away. I then stepped forward to perform the ceremony. (I must say I delivered my lines quite well!) As they took their vows to love and honor each other, I maintained marvelous control —I didn't puddle up once! Later at the reception, many people came up to me and marveled, "Doctor Schuller, you were so relaxed! You seem to be enjoying all this." "Absolutely," I replied, "I decided I would enjoy it, after all I was paying the bill!" So I had a wonderful time.

I think the reason why it was such a super event for me is because it underscored the fact that I am a success in the most important area of my life. Some people might question my success as a clergyman, or a pastor, or an author. But nobody can debate the fact that I am a success as a husband and a father!

The Tassel Is Worth the Hassle

My son, who was a student at Fuller Theological Seminary, graduated from my alma mater, Hope College in Holland, Michigan, seven years ago. The moment he received his B.A. degree was one of the proudest moments of my life. I watched as he received his diploma and moved the tassel on his mortarboard from the left side to the right.

After the ceremony we met outside. Beaming with delight, we hugged each other and slapped one another on the back. "You made it!" I exclaimed. "Yes," he said, grinning broadly. "I made it. But it was tough." "But it was worth it, though, wasn't it?" I asked. "It was worth it," he repeated. "But at times I wondered. It was quite a hassle." As he spoke those words, my eyes were drawn to the tassel flowing from his cap. Touching it lightly, I said, "The tassel is worth the hassle." "You bet!" my son affirmed enthusiastically.

If you make your decisions based upon how comfortable, easy, convenient, or painless your choices are, then don't ever expect great rewards. Hassle-free living is tassel-free living. You can be sure that the tassel is in proportion to the hassle. Pay a big price and you can expect a good return!

Hassles Can Help You Grow

Do you remember the story of the little boy who stormed angrily home from his first day at kindergarten? "How did you like school?" his mother asked gently. "I didn't like it," he replied sulkily. "In fact," he continued, "I not only didn't like it, I'm quitting!" "You're quitting!" his mother exclaimed incredulously. "Why, you can't do that!" "I don't care if I can or I can't," the little boy said. "I'm quitting." "Why do you want to quit school?" she questioned. "Look, Mom," the child replied, "school is an awful place. I can't write. I don't know how to read. And they wouldn't let me talk. There's nothing to it, so I quit!"

Personal growth comes when we learn through our hassles what our potential capabilities and capacities for learning really are. Hassles show us how we can grow.

A Glorious Impossibility

Not long ago I heard on television an interview with one of the runners in the Boston Marathon. "Why did you run the race?" the young woman asked. "I know you weren't paid for it. Was the race a physically pleasurable experience?" "No," the runner answered. "As a matter of fact, it was pretty painful —especially the last few hills."

Running can be painful, but it can also be sheer joy. This morning I rose before dawn and went out on the road to run a few miles. I experienced a wonderful feeling. As I ran through the silent neighborhood, I felt that I was alive and the rest of the world was dead and hadn't resurrected yet. I had eyes that could see the drifting clouds and the sun as it struggled to break over the horizon, while the sleepers were blind as they huddled under their warm sheets in their darkened bedrooms. I could hear the sound of the birds singing and the light breeze softly ruffling the leaves of the trees, while they were deaf to the music of an awakening world. I could feel strength building through my veins, I could feel strength building and energy flowing through my limbs. I was alive!

But I must admit, not every morning is like that. Some days it's difficult to drag myself from bed and run those miles in the early morning. And, like the marathon runner, I often find that pushing myself to the limits of my endurance can be a less than pleasurable experience. So I listened with anticipation when the reporter pressed the marathoner to tell why he had subjected himself to that grueling twenty-six-mile race. The runner said, "I ran the race because of the glorious impossibility of it." Until we are faced with a glorious impossibility, we don't know what we are, who we are, or what we can do.

Hidden Treasure

As I recall my visits to the shimmering emerald waters which surround the Greek peninsula, I remember a tour into the hinterlands of that country.

My guide took me through some of the glorious temples built in the age of Pericles some 2,360 years ago. As he gestured toward the empty marble pedestals in and around the temple grounds, he explained, "On these pedestals once stood some of the most beautiful pieces of marble sculpture ever created in the Ancient World. Most of them were lost when the Romans invaded Greece. These works of art were carted down to Roman ships—many of which were lost at sea."

Greece's most magnificent treasures now lie hidden under the waters of the Mediterranean. Like the talents and treasures that lie within you, they are just waiting to be discovered.

Gold of Glacier Bay

If you've ever had the opportunity to journey up into the far north near Glacier Bay, you know it's a spectacular experience. Glacier Bay is located in a region so far from civilization that it is as primitive, virginal, and unspoiled as the dawn of creation. There are no cars, houses, or neon lights for as far as the eye can see. I took a tour of the bay by ship. As we approached the three-hundred-foot high, sheer cliff of diamond-blue ice, we heard it creak and groan Then suddenly the cliff splintered from top to bottom and, with a screeching crack and deafening snap, a huge chunk of this millenniums-old glacier slid thunderously into the ocean and exploded in white foam. The echo of the explosion reverberated through the hills of the desolate countryside.

Many geologists feel certain that, as this river of

frozen ice scoured the bottom and sides of the valleys through the centuries, it carried with it vast, unknown amounts of precious metals. Within that glacier may be the largest, purest gold nugget that has ever been created! It simply hasn't been uncovered yet!

Could there be a gold nugget within you that you haven't yet discovered?

Bear Quarterback Finds Religion

Once someone sent me an article from the *Chicago Tribune*. The headline read BEAR QUARTERBACK FINDS RELIGION—EVANS' LIFE CHANGES OFF THE FIELD TOO. The story told of how Vince Evans, quarterback for the Chicago Bears, had suddenly developed a tremendous sense of self-confidence and was showing remarkable potential. In the previous few weeks, he had thrown more than his share of touchdown passes. He had suddenly begun to develop his potential for greatness. In short, he was worshiping God in the beauty of holiness which, for him, was playing great football.

What made the difference? He was suddenly inspired by a new idea. Anytime you act upon a great new idea, you are going to become a different person. What new idea inspired Vince Evans? According to Evans, something happened the previous Easter that made him more confident. "I was looking at Reverend Robert Schuller of Garden Grove, California, on television," said Evans. "I've watched him before because he talks about positive thinking. He was talking about the Resurrection. It was cloudy at that particular time. Just as he said Jesus had risen, the sun came out.

"My television is on a loft under a skylight. The sun shone in and beamed on my face. I knew Jesus Christ had come into my life and I overflowed with tears. I was always religiously inclined, but I never had a personal relationship with God until then." The rest of the story told how Vince Evans now lets his faith make a difference in his attitude toward daily life.

Worship the Lord in the beauty of holiness. Be daring and courageous enough to open up to beautiful new ideas. When you do, a lot of things are going to open up to you.

Cut the Motor

One morning I took a motorboat ride across the Sea of Galilee. Suddenly, in the middle of the lake, the operator of the boat cut the motor, and I wondered for a moment if we were out of gas. When I inquired, he said, "No. I thought it would be nice, Doctor Schuller, if you could just listen to the quietness out here." Soon the boat stopped rocking and the only sounds we heard were the sounds of the water lapping gently against the stern and the majestic silence of the centuries, as we sat in the very same sea Jesus fished nearly two thousand years ago.

There must come a time in each of our lives when

we cut the motor, stop the boat, and just pause to be still and recognize the mighty presence of God. Most of us allows ourselves to get into a rut. We think we know the answers to all the important questions in our lives. We think we have our philosophies, ideologies, theology, and psychology all neatly packaged and labeled. When we feel safe and secure in our knowledge, when we think we have all the answers, then it's time to stop the motor and ask ourselves, "Am I ready for a new idea?"

Boiled Peanuts

I tried something this week I want to share with you. I was in Georgia to give a lecture. While being driven to the lecture hall, I saw little roadside stands all along the way which read BOILED PEANUTS FOR SALE. I had never heard of boiled peanuts before, so I asked my driver about them.

"You've never had boiled peanuts?" my driver asked incredulously. "No," I replied, "do they actually boil them?" "Sure," he said. "Be adventuresome. Try them." So he pulled over to the side of the road, and I followed him to one of the stands where there was a big pot of boiling water. Floating on the surface like sea kelp were peanuts still in their shells. The man took a dipper and scooped the soggy peanuts up into a paper bag.

When I returned to the car, I went to crack the nut and water squirted me in the nose. When I finally got it out of the shell and into my mouth, I discovered it really was very good. I feel I must commend Georgia and President Carter for giving us boiled peanuts.

But when I went to hand the bag of peanuts to my friend in the front seat, the bottom dropped out and all the peanuts landed in my lap.

It's fun to try something new. But what is really fun is when the new thing you try really puts beauty into your life. What we all need are beautiful ideas. And Jesus Christ is my idea of a beautiful idea.

The Glorious Buffet

This summer I was traveling with my wife and our two youngest daughters. We were the guests of a company up north where I spoke, and they provided accommodations for us at a lovely hotel. The first morning I was there, I arose early and went out on my usual morning run. On the way back to my room, I saw the buffet table. It was glorious—piled high with everything imaginable: fruit, all kinds of meats, eggs, fish, blueberry and bran muffins, pancakes, waffles, and French toast. Although I usually shy away from big breakfasts, I decided to indulge that morning.

When I returned to our room, I found our daughter Gretchen cuddled up in our bed dozing peacefully. "Gretchen," I said, "come on out! Let's go to breakfast!" "Nope," she answered, "I'm ordering room service." "Gretchen, do you know what you get here for room service?" I asked. "Yes," she said, "Breakfast in bed. I've never had breakfast in bed, and today I'm going to." "But Gretchen," I argued, "all you get from room service is cold cereal and

milk." "I like cold cereal and milk," she answered.
"I want breakfast in bed."

"Gretchen," I exclaimed, "you should see the
buffet table! They have scrambled eggs [her
favorite], bacon, French toast. . . ." And she pulled
the covers over her head. She didn't want to hear.
"Gretchen," I continued, "they also have blueberry
muffins." And she pulled a pillow over her head.
"They have bran muffins and pancakes, too," I
shouted, as she buried her head deeper into the
pillows and pulled a second blanket over her head.
She didn't want to hear, because hearing meant
changing her way of thinking. Hearing meant getting
out of a comfortable bed, getting dressed, and going
down into the dining room—something she wasn't
prepared to do.

You may be missing a super banquet—the banquet
of love, joy, and peace of mind you could be enjoying through a relationship with Jesus Christ.
Make the necessary changes, get ready to wake up
and embrace Jesus Christ. Accept the banquet He of-
fers you. Dare to try something you never have tried
before.

A Hole in the Boat

We had a staff meeting some months ago, and during
that meeting I drew a sketch of an oceanliner with
about seven different stories. At the top level was the
captain, looking at the splendid view. The next level
was the lounge, where people were having intimate
conversation. At the next level were people enjoying

the excellent cuisine. The next level was the sundeck, where people were sunning themselves. And finally you came to the cabin area. Way at the bottom in one end was the theater, and at the other end was the engine room. And next to the engine room, just slightly above the mechanical room, was a little room called the washroom. In it were automatic washers and automatic dryers. This room happened to be run by one simple fellow who was getting sick and tired of all the rich tourists who used the washroom and ran off with the towels. And nobody paid attention to him. He was forgotten, isolated, and abandoned. Even the people who came to use this little room didn't listen to his rules.

Finally he decided that he was not going to stand for it anymore, so he got a hammer and some nails and hammered the towels to the wall. "Now they won't run off with my towels!" he said. The captain, who couldn't have cared less, didn't know about it. The people up in the bar and in the restaurant and the people sunning themselves really didn't care. Nobody cared what the little fellow did with his towels. If he wanted to hammer them to the wall, then he could just go ahead.

But what the man who hammered the towels to the wall didn't know was that it was an outside wall. He had never seen the ship blueprints. But suddenly the water was leaking in. He jammed it with a bar of soap, and that just dissolved. He stuck his fingers in the hole, but that didn't seem to be the most fruitful solution to the problem. And finally, in desperation and hysteria, he pulled his fingers out and the water was up to his ankles. It would only be a matter of time before the captain was going to be concerned about some little fellow who hammered the towels to the wall of the ship.

The real point is, *a hole in a boat is a hole in a boat*. All human beings who live on planet earth are on the same ship, spinning at an incredible speed through space. We can take an I-don't-care attitude like the captain at the top towards the little man in the washroom. We can take that kind of an attitude towards other people in other states, other professions, other races and nationalities. But you can be sure a hole in a boat is a hole in a boat is a hole in a boat.

The Americans and Their Houseboy

Four servicemen, who were assigned to the East Coast, were given living quarters and a private houseboy who would take care of their laundry, make up their beds, and clean their room. Well, these young American soldiers loved pranks, so they decided to pull a joke on the fellow.

The first night on the base they waited until he was asleep and then one of the GI's slipped out of bed and went into his room. Then he carefully proceeded to nail his shoes to the wooden floor. The next morning they were awakened with a knock at the door. When they opened the door, there was the houseboy. "Good morning," the aide said. They looked down and saw that he was wearing his shoes. He was carrying a tray and on it were four cups of black, thick, hot, steaming coffee. "Here's your coffee," he enthused without saying another word. And so, the four servicemen drank their coffee.

The next night the Americans decided to pull another prank and put sand in the houseboy's bed. The following morning there was a knock on the door. One of the men opened it, and there was the aide once again. They expected him to be very angry, but he was smiling again, "Good morning," he said, holding the tray with hot, thick, black steaming coffee. He didn't even hint that he had a bad night of sleep.

Well, the young men couldn't take it. They couldn't stand pulling pranks on such a nice fellow. They felt so bad, so repentant, and so remorseful that they called him in and told him to sit down. "Look, we're very sorry," they explained. "We have been very mean and rude to you. We're very sorry that we nailed your shoes to the floor, and we're sorry we put sand in your bed last night. We are not going to play any more pranks on you ever again, you are just too nice." He smiled. "You no more nail my shoes to the floor?" "No," they answered in unison. "You no more put sand in my bed?" "No," they answered again, "Okay. Then me no more put mud in your coffee."

Everything we do provokes an action or reaction from someone. You and I are either part of the problem or part of the solution.

The Sanctified Hypocrite

Henry Fawcett was one of the great distinguished members of Parliament in England. William Gladstone appointed him Postmaster General, and he made one of the greatest contributions to England in the whole area of the postal services and telegraphy. The story behind it is this: Henry Fawcett was blind! He had every reason to be bitter. It happened when he was twenty years old. He and his dad had a super relationship. One day they were out hunting, and the father accidentally discharged the gun and shot his son in the face. This bright, healthy, mentally alert young boy of twenty dropped, covered with blood. The father rushed over to his son's side and took him home. The boy lived, but he was sightless the rest of his life. The father wanted to kill himself. And young Henry wanted to die, too. He had no hope, for he would not be able to read again. He would not be able to study or go back to school. All of these negative thoughts went through his mind over and over again.

Then one day he overheard his father crying. He was swearing out loud and condemning himself for ruining his son's life. This was when Henry decided to build his father's hopes. He would pretend! "It's okay, Dad," Henry said. "Don't worry, I'll soon learn to read. Others can read to me." But in his heart it was a lie. So only to keep his father from self-destruction, young Henry Fawcett lived a lie of laughter, and optimism, and enthusiasm. He lived the life of joy. But he didn't have joy; he didn't have enthusiasm. He was, you might say, a sanctified hypocrite.

But then something happened. There came a moment when the lie became a reality! The act became the real thing! The play became the truth! He had hope! And his hope produced results! And results produced progress! He began, you see, to listen to his own positive statements, even when he didn't mean them.

Bright Faces

Edward Rosenow was one of the great doctors at the Mayo Clinic for many years. His career as a doctor really started for him when he was a little boy, living in Minnesota. His brother was critically ill, so his parents called for the doctor. He said, "I'll never forget when the doctor came to the house. My father's and my mother's faces were strained with fear and worry. The doctor told them to wait with me around the table in the dining room while he went into the bedroom and closed the door. He seemed to be gone a very long time. I looked at my dad and his face was dark. I looked at my mother and her face was dark. When the doctor came out of the bedroom and closed the door, he looked at each of us for a moment and his face broke into a smile. "You can relax, folks, he's going to be all right!" Young Ed said, "At that time I saw a light come into my dad's face, and a light come into my mother's face. And I decided then and there I was going to be a doctor when I grew up, because I wanted to put light in people's faces."

There's a calling for you! There's a plan and a dream for you! Every life is to be a light.

The Bridge of Moses

I'm reminded of a story about a little boy who came home from Sunday school, bragging about how good the class was, so his mother said, "What did you learn today?" And the boy replied, "I learned how Moses got the Israelites out of Egypt." "How did he do it?" the mother prodded. "Very simply," he continued, "Moses hired some bridge experts and they built a suspension bridge ten times as long as the Golden Gate Bridge. It went clear across the Red Sea!" "That's hard to believe," his mother laughed. "Look," the persistent child said, "if I told you what they really taught me, you'd *never* believe me!"

Motivate Me

Be motivated! Like the story of the little boy whose mother was a psychologist, and he came to the breakfast table one morning, refusing to eat his cereal. She tried all of the manipulative tactics, but nothing worked. She tried all of the tricks of behavioral modification, but none of it worked. Finally she lost her cool and yelled at him. He looked coolly across the table and said, "Motivate me!" How do you motivate people? God uses impossible situations to motivate persons. God deliberately throws mountains in front of us, so we'll fall on our knees and ask for help!

A Brand-New Car

A funny thing happened to me this morning on the way to church. I was driving the old car that I bought seven years ago. It's been such a faithful old car. A few miles from church, I looked down at the speedometer and watched the little blocks change: 99,999.5 . . . 99,999.6 . . . 99,999.7 . . . 99,999.8 . . . 99,999.9 . . .—then the odometer read 00,000.0, and I had a brand-new car!

Now we all know that you cannot tell the newness of a car by the odometer, and you can't tell a book by its cover. That's not a new car just because the odometer reads 00,000.0! That car can't be recreated into a brand-new car, but *you* can be recreated into a brand-new person! You can become a totally new creature, if you will let Jesus Christ come into your life.

A Courageous Woman

In 1921, Lewis Lawes became the warden at Sing Sing Prison. No prison was tougher than Sing Sing during that time. But when Warden Lawes retired twenty some years later, that prison had become a humanitarian institution. It was a model for other prisons to follow. Those who studied the system said credit for the change belonged to Lewis Lawes. But when Warden Lawes was asked about the transformation, this is what he said: "I owe it all to my wonderful wife, Catherine, who is buried outside the prison walls."

Catherine Lawes was a young mother with three small children when her husband became the warden at Sing Sing prison. Everybody warned her from the beginning that she should never step foot inside the prison walls or in any other facility that the prisoners would be using, but that didn't stop Catherine! When the first prison basketball game was held, she insisted on going. She walked into the auditorium with her three beautiful children and sat in the stands with the hard-core criminals. Other guests came up to her afterwards and asked, "How do you dare sit with these men? Why do you take your little children in there?" And her reply was, "My husband and I are going to take care of these men, and I believe they will take care of me! I don't have to worry!"

She even insisted on getting acquainted with the records of the men. She discovered that one of the men convicted of murder was blind, so she paid him a visit. She stepped into the cold cell and sat down next to this man. Holding his hand in hers she warmly said, "Do you read Braille?" "What's Braille?" he asked. "Don't you know? It is a way that you can read with your fingers," she explained. "Well, I've never heard of it," he replied. "I'll teach you then!" she enthused. And she taught that blind killer how to read Braille. Years later he would weep in love for her.

Later Catherine found that there was a deaf-mute in the prison, so she went to school to learn sign language. Soon she was communicating with him through the use of her hands. Many said that Catherine Lawes was the body of Jesus Christ that came alive again at Sing Sing prison from 1921 to 1937.

Then one evening the car in which she was riding went out of control, and she was killed. The next morning her husband did not come to work, so the acting warden came in his place. In an instant, the whole prison knew something was wrong. When they heard the news that their beloved lady had died, everyone wept.

The following day her body was resting in a casket in her home, three-quarters of a mile from the prison. As the acting warden took his early-morning walk, he was shocked to see a large crowd of the toughest, hardest-looking criminals, gathering like a herd of animals at the main gate. It looked as if they were ready to launch a riot. He walked over to the group and, instead of seeing hostility in their eyes, he saw tears of grief and sadness. He knew how much they loved and admired Catherine. He turned and faced the men. "All right, men, you can go. Just be sure and check in tonight!" Then he opened the gate without another word and a parade of more than one hundred criminals walked, without a guard, three-quarters of a mile to stand in line to pay their respects to Catherine Lawes. And every one of them checked in that night. *Every one! It's amazing what one life can do when it has the Spirit of Christ within.* Catherine Lawes believed there were no hopeless cases, only hopeless thinkers!

The warden's wife had the courage to take her little children and sit among murderers and rapists. Do you have courage? How much nerve do you have? Do you have enough courage to trust God as He comes to you and says: "I believe in you! I have a dream for your life!"

The Hands of Christ

In a small French country village during World War II, there was a beautiful marble statue of Jesus with His hands outstretched before him, standing in the courtyard of a quaint little church. One day a bomb struck too close, and the statue was dismembered. After the battle was over and the enemy had passed through, the citizens of the village decided to find the pieces of their beloved statue and reconstruct it. It was no work of art by Michelangelo or Bernini, but it was a part of their lives, and they loved it just the same. And so they gathered the broken pieces and reassembled it. Even the scars on the body added to its beauty. But there was one problem. They were unable to find the hands of the statue. "A Christ without hands is no Christ at all," someone lamented. "Hands with scars—yes. But what's a Lord without hands? We need a new statue." Then someone else came along with another idea, and it prevailed. A brass plaque was attached at the base of the statue which reads I HAVE NO HANDS BUT YOUR HANDS.

The Three Pennies of Sister Theresa

Sister Theresa had a dream one day. She told her superiors, "I have three pennies and a dream from God to build an orphanage." "Sister Theresa," her superiors chided gently, "you cannot build an orphanage with three pennies. With three pennies, you can't do anything." "I know," she said, smiling, "but with God and three pennies, I *can* do anything!"

Don't Miss the Positives

There was once a professor who took a piece of paper and pinned it on the board in his classroom. Then with a felt-tip pen he made a circle and colored it in with black. When he finished, he asked his psychology class, "What do you see?" One person said, "A black dot." Another person said, "I see a round circle and it's dark." Another one said, "I see a round circle colored solid black." And so he went through the class, until finally the professor said, "Doesn't anybody see a piece of white paper?" They all picked out the black dot. Nobody pointed to the white sheet of paper.

Most of the people you work with and live with are negative people. They look at the faults; they pick out the shortcomings; they point out the defects; they show the imperfections; they spot the flaws; they focus on the wrinkles; they check the stains; they look for the negatives. They miss everything that's positive and great.

Life Can Be Great at Ninety-Eight

This past week I talked to a beautiful gentleman. This man was one of the most inspiring men I have ever met. He was not exactly young when I met him last year. Six months earlier he had celebrated his ninety-eighth birthday. But what a chipper old fellow he is! He works six days a week in his factory, operating America's last hand-hewn-copper-kettle factory. What a bright and alert man!

I knew people who, when they get older, don't like birthdays. They are always complaining about getting old. I love birthdays! You know why? Because if I didn't have a birthday every year, I wouldn't be here! That's what you call a positive attitude. I asked my friend, "How long are you going to live?" Smiling, he said, "Oh, I'm planning to live to one hundred!" "Wow!" I exclaimed. "How can I live to be one hundred?" "Very simple," he enthused, "anybody can live to be one hundred. All you do is live to be ninety-nine—and then be *very* careful!"

When I saw my friend this time, it happened to be a very unpleasant day for me, and I made some negative comment about it. He looked me in the eye and said, "Doctor Schuller, every day is a good day!

Every day is better than no day at all!'' Think of that. *Every day is better than no day at all!*

Ninety-eight years old and a great believer in God and possibility thinking! Some people look upon the years as burdens. My ninety-eight-year-old friend looks upon every added year as another blessing. It's all a matter of your mental attitude. And you have the freedom to choose how you will think!

The Courage of Hubert Humphrey

I first met Hubert Humphrey in 1971. I received a letter from him saying that he and his wife, Muriel, watched the ''Hour of Power'' and that it was a great help to them on a very deep and personal level. He told me to stop in and see him the next time I was in Washington, so I did! When I found his office, I told his secretary who I was and she smiled and said, ''Oh, Doctor Schuller, he really wants to see you!'' Then she had a member of his staff take me to the Senate Chamber where Senator Humphrey was speaking.

He was finishing, just as I entered the room. When he rushed over and warmly embraced me, I didn't know exactly what to say, so I handed him one of the little gold cards with the possibility-thinkers' creed printed on it. ''What's this?'' Hubert asked. And I told him to read it. In his strong and sturdy voice, he began reading:

When faced with a mountain I will not quit, I will keep on striving until I climb over, find a pass through, tunnel underneath or simply stay and turn the mountain into a gold mine, with God's help.

Tears filled his eyes before he could finish. This was only the beginning of what would become a deep, personal relationship.

People have said it through the years and I affirm it today—Hubert Humphrey had great courage! People who fight a terminal illness, and keep on fighting bravely, have courage! I have always admired their perseverance. I have always admired their faith. But I used to say, "Why do you call it courage? What's so brave about it? Perseverance? Yes. Toughness? Of course. But courageousness? But why do you say it's *courageous,* when somebody's fighting a battle of cancer?"

It's courageous because a person who fights a brave battle with a terminal illness, is making a commitment! There can be no courage unless there is a choice between alternatives. And the person who is fighting a terminal illness is making a choice between two alternatives. One is to overdose and slip away quickly. The other is to hang in there as bravely and optimistically as possible, until God stops the heartbeat. When you're faced with alternatives, you choose the one where the personal price is high but the rewards in terms of inspiration to those around you is high. That's *courage!*

Dear Abby, "What's Wrong With Suicide?"

In my latest book, *Peace of Mind Through Possibility Thinking,* I tell about a conversation I had with a good friend—Abby. She writes her own syndicated newspaper column called "Dear Abby." We were at dinner together in Beverly Hills, and I was telling her about our ministry and the suicides that we prevent through our twenty-four-hour life-line telephone Christian counseling program. She was surprised when I told her that we operate the longest-standing, continually operating New Hope Telephone Counseling Center right here on the campus of the Garden Grove Community Church. I told her how proud we were of the fact that no ministry saves more lives than we do!

Abby's reply was a question: "Dr. Schuller, what's so wrong about suicide?" "What's wrong with suicide," I replied, "is that your friends and relatives are left behind to live with the terrible hurt! They are the ones who must carry the scars for the rest of their lives!"

Your life and mine will be judged before Almighty God on this question: "When I was faced with alternatives, did I choose the brave way?" And if I did, I uplifted the collective level of social self-esteem in the process.

Charlotte Valente

I have never met Charlotte Valente but I surely want to some day. I became acquainted with her story through some literature I received from the Children's Hospital in Los Angeles. Mary Ames Anderson, now the retired editor, said if she were to pick one child in the Children's Hospital who inspired her more than anybody else, it would have to be Charlotte Valente. And here's Mary Anderson's beautiful story.

"I was walking through the corridor of the Children's Hospital in 1953, when I heard a young voice say, 'Here I am!' I stopped and turned to see where the voice was coming from. And that's when I saw a little girl, barely two years old, lying in bed hugging her teddy bear. She seemed so young to be speaking so clearly. Both of her tiny legs were hanging in the air, in traction. 'Well, hello!' I enthused. Smiling, she asked, 'How are you today?' But before I could answer, she interrupted, 'I have brittle bones. This one is broken. Last time it was that one,' she said, as she pointed to her right leg. 'But this time it is this one. I have had eleven fractures!'

"By the age of six Charlotte had been in and out of the hospital eighty-five times. She has a rare disease, which makes her bones break very easily. She had over two hundred fractures by the time she was ten, but she was a delightful little girl, always smiling and very positive.

"I only saw her cry twice," Mrs. Anderson wrote. "Once when she fractured her arm the day before her sister's wedding, and she had to stay in the hospital. The other time was when she made a community appeal to urge people to give so crippled children could walk. 'I will never walk,' Charlotte said in her plea, 'but hundreds of others can walk if only you'll help!' Charlotte couldn't walk because by the time she reached puberty, the disease had arrested itself. Her normal development had been permanently distorted. She would probably never weigh more than fifty pounds in her entire lifetime. But this brave young girl didn't cry until she was recognized by community leaders. And do you know why? Because they gave her a typewriter—the one material thing that she'd wanted ever since she was a child. She didn't want a bike, because she could never ride one. She wanted a typewriter! And when she was presented this gift, she cried and cried. 'I'm the luckiest girl in the whole world!' she exclaimed."

Charlotte went on to high school and graduated. Then she picked a university that had ramps equipped for the handicapped. She was accepted and graduated four years later cum laude! But Charlotte did not stop there! She went on to law school and passed the state bar exam. All fifty pounds of her!

The Ideal One

The late Ozzie Nelson used to tell this story about a friend of his son Ricky.

He said, "Ricky was just a young boy when he begged me to let his friend Walter come over and spend the weekend with him. And after much persistence, I gave in. On the day that Walter was to come over, I got off work a little early, so I could play with the boys. We went into the backyard and started throwing a football around. I was getting really good, when Ricky said, 'Hey, Dad, you're great!' And Walter piped in and exclaimed, 'Gee, Mr. Nelson, you've got a pretty good arm, but not as good as my dad.' When it came to dinner time I carved the roast so beautifully with thin and even slices. 'Look at those nice slices, Walter,' I bragged. 'You carve the roast pretty good, Mr. Nelson,' Walter enthused, 'but you should see my dad do it!' I couldn't believe it! I couldn't do anything as well as this kid's father.

"Well, when their bedtime came I decided to tell one of my best stories. Their eyes were popping out of their heads! 'That's a great story, Mr. Nelson, but my dad is one of the best storytellers there is!' And the next day the same thing happened—no matter what we did together. I was starting to dislike a man I'd never even met. I couldn't wait for Walter's mother to pick him up, so I could find out about this superdad! When she came to the door, I said, 'Hi! I'm delighted to meet you.' 'How was Walter?' she asked. 'Oh, just great,' I exclaimed. 'I'd sure like to meet your husband. He must be something else!' 'Oh, no!' she said, 'has Walter been talking about his dad again? You see, Walter was only three years old when his dad was killed at Corregidor.' " That little boy had an Ideal One who lived within him.

My Ideal One died before I was born—at Calvary! His name is Jesus! That's where I get my courage. That's where I get my nerve. He lives in me and He wants to live in you!

Dr. Henry Poppen

A visit to Hong Kong brought back some beautiful memories of a good friend, Dr. Henry Poppen. He was on my staff for many years, until he went to be with the Lord at the age of eighty-three. Dr. Poppen was one of the first missionaries to go to China. After spending over forty years there, he was called into public trial in the main city square. Over ten thousand people jammed the square as accusation after accusation was read against him. Finally, he was declared guilty on all counts and told he must leave the country.

Dr. Poppen and his wife boarded a bus and headed to Swatow, hoping to board a steamer and leave for freedom in Hong Kong, and then back to America. But in Swatow, Henry was pulled off the bus, brought to solitary confinement and confined to a little cell, six feet by eight feet. The ceiling was so low, he couldn't stand up straight. He didn't know what was going to happen to him, but he did know that most missionaries who were prisoners of Mao Tsetung never lived to tell about it.

Mrs. Poppen was put on a train, then a boat, and finally found herself in Hong Kong. She waited anxiously in a hotel, not knowing where her beloved husband was.

Dr. Poppen spent hour after hour, and day by day in his small, dark cell. After four and a half days, he could stand the blackness and the mental torture no more. At midnight he got on his hands and knees by his small wooden cot and prayed, "Oh, God, you know I am not Saint Paul, or the Apostle John or

Saint Peter. I am only Henry Poppen, and Henry Poppen can take no more! Lord, open the door!"

He fell asleep on his hands and knees, only to be awakened about an hour later by the creaking of the hinges on his cell door. The guards came in and tied a rope around his neck with a slipknot, ran it down his backbone and bound his arms behind him so tightly that if he struggled at all, he would strangle himself. Then they led him down a dark, winding cobblestone street, until he saw the reflection of light in rippling water. He heard the hum and chunking of an engine. Then he saw the dark outline of an ocean steamer, waiting, with its gangplank down. The guards shoved him onto the deck and said, "Now get out of our country!"

The gangplank was raised, and the steamer blew the whistle. The captain took the rope off his neck and cut it loose from his hands. Dr. Poppen raised his proud head, a free man under God! The gift of an open door—what greater gift can God give you than that? God heard Dr. Poppen's prayer, and He opened the door and delivered him! The power of positive prayer.

Three Little Whacks

I'm reminded of a story Mary Goforth's father told in one of his books. There was a young woodpecker who was given training on how to properly go about drilling holes in trees. He was taught the correct method to throw his head back to achieve maximum thrust. He learned how to sharpen his beak to a perfect point on the bark of a tree. And, being the determined woodpecker that he was, he graduated in the top 10 percent of his class.

As a new graduate, he was given his first assignment and his instructors pointed him to an appropriate tree. With extreme confidence, this cocky young woodpecker stretched his wings and flew to the assigned tree. Grabbing hold of the bark with his sturdy feet, he inspected the wood and, as he had been taught to do, threw back his head and took his first whack. A chip of bark flew from the trunk of the tree and the eyes of the woodpecker sparkled with pride—finally he was doing what he was meant to do. Again he threw back his head and took another whack. This time an even larger piece of wood flew from the tree. He was doing great. Then, just as he threw his head back and took his third whack at the tree, lightning struck, splintering the trunk into fragments, and sending the woodpecker tumbling to the ground.

Dazed, but not seriously hurt, the young woodpecker flew with feeble wings to a tree adjoining the one he had been working on so industriously. He looked at the splintered tree trunk and said incredulously, "Wow! To think I did it with only three little whacks!"

Most likely our difficult situations will not be solved with "three little whacks" of our own. We as human beings simply aren't that smart. But if we're really in tune with God and His will, He intervenes in our lives. Only He can know what great things we can accomplish with Him.

The Skeptic

Here's a funny story that illustrates lack of faith.

The Japanese are famous for their skill with computers. Recently they installed a fully computerized scale which, instead of giving you a ticker-tape readout of your height and weight, gives you personal data via a mechanical voice.

A skeptical American dropped in a coin and out of the speaker of this inventive Japanese device came the following announcement: YOU ARE AN AMERICAN. YOU ARE 5'10" TALL. YOU WEIGH 185 LBS. AND YOU ARE BOOKED ON FLIGHT 408 TO LOS ANGELES, CALIFORNIA. The man was totally incredulous. He was sure someone was playing some kind of practical joke on him. So he sneaked back into the club lounge, changed his clothes, put on a different coat, and pulled his hat over his ears, so that it hid his face. Hobbling like a shrunken old man, the American stepped onto the machine, dropped in his dime, and waited for the announcement. YOU ARE AN AMERICAN, the voice announced from the speaker. YOU ARE 5'10" TALL. YOU WEIGH 185 LBS. AND WHILE YOU WERE CHANGING YOUR CLOTHES, YOUR PLANE LEFT FOR LOS ANGELES.

Any counselor will tell you that it is very difficult for people who naturally employ manipulative avoidance reaction response or intentional inattention to believe.

The Child With an Exceptional Future

Yesterday I met with a young couple who came to visit our church campus from a city far away. They were a beautiful couple—a happy husband and wife, and in her arms, the young woman held a beautiful little baby boy. As we stood together outside the Tower of Hope, they said to me, "Doctor Schuller, this ministry has given us real faith—faith that can turn our scars into stars. It's made us strong for our little boy." And I looked at the darling little three-month-old baby boy, sleeping in the blanket. "May I hold him?" I asked. As I held the warm, sleeping bundle, I wondered what they could have meant—what scars could this small child have put upon their lives?

But without my asking, they explained, "You see, Doctor Schuller, we just got word that both of our child's little legs must be amputated below the knee. He was born without bones between the knee and ankle. God really used your daughter Carol's accident to help us see a bright future for him. You gave us faith. We know he's going to be an exceptional child with an exceptional future." And we held hands and prayed together and claimed God's promise in Jeremiah 29:11: "I have a plan for your life. It is a plan for good and not evil. It is a plan to give you a future with hope."

George W. Campbell

George W. Campbell was born blind. When he was a child, there was no cure for the disease known as congenital bilateral cataracts. The doctor said to the father, "At this time, there is absolutely no cure. He will be destined to be sightless all of his life." The child grew and learned to walk, laugh, sing, and play. At six years of age something happened. He was playing with a friend who had forgotten for a moment that he was sightless. The friend threw the ball at him and saw that it was headed straight for his little face. The friend shouted, "George, look out! It's going to hit you!" The ball hit him in the face. He went to his mother and said, "How did Roy know something was going to happen to me before it happened?"

His mother sat down and took his little hands in hers. She counted his fingers and began, "George, I want to tell you something: People have five senses. The thumb stands for hearing; you can hear me talk to you. This little finger stands for touching; you can feel me touch you. This little finger stands for the tongue; you can taste food. And this little finger stands for smelling; you can smell when I bake bread. And this little finger stands for seeing." Then she took that little finger and with a rope she tied it into the palm of his hand. She said, "George, you're different from other people. With you this little finger doesn't work. You cannot see. But now you have four fingers and I've got the other one tied down. I want you to put both of your hands out and I'm going to throw a ball to you. Catch it; here it comes!"

He caught it and she explained, "See, George! I want you to know that as you grow up, you can catch a ball, even though you're missing one finger. You can catch hold of life and live a full and wonderful life, even though you cannot see." And that beautiful, positive possibility placed in his little life made him a positive, creative, and fruitful person.

At age eighteen he was sick in the hospital with a minor ailment, when the news came out that a treatment had been discovered that might be helpful to congenital bilateral cataracts. It was risky, but the father determined after discussing it with George that it was worth the risk. So they performed two surgeries on each eye over a six-month period of time.

During this long period of surgeries, they were prayerful and hopeful. When the last surgery was complete and the bandages were removed, the doctor asked, "George, do you see anything?" He could only see what seemed like a dull blur, so he was still considered legally blind. And then something happened. He heard a voice over his face saying, "George, this is your mother. Can you see?" The blur turned into a color, the color took shape, and suddenly he, for the first time in his life, saw a human face. It was the face of a sixty-two-year-old woman, wrinkled, with white hair. When he was old, he said, "It was the first face I ever saw—and was it ever beautiful." He didn't see her wrinkles. He didn't see the old lines that had begun to form. He didn't notice that her hands were gnarled and old. They were the hands that had held his little hands. This was the voice that had spoken to him all those years. This was his mother. He lived a normal and beautiful life and he said, "The most beautiful moment of my life was when my eyes were opened, and I saw the face of my mother."

There are many of you who know what I'm talking about. Do you remember when your eyes were first opened to the possibilities that God had locked up for you? The most beautiful moment in life is when your eyes are opened and you see the face of Jesus. When you became a possibility thinker and stopped being a negative thinker, you discovered the potential of power within yourself. I believe God is going to do something in your life, and you'll see what you have not seen before and will never forget it.

Mine Your Mind

One Saturday morning I was on a plane flight to Los Angeles and I had to work on my Sunday-morning message. I was not in the mood to communicate with the person who sat next to me—not because I'm unfriendly, but because I have only limited hours left, and nobody else is going to prepare my brain for Sunday morning. My suitcase was open; one of my books was there; and my picture was on the back of the jacket. The man who sat next to me saw it, looked at me, and interrupted my solitude, saying, "Are you an author?" I said, "Yes." He said, "So am I." Then he asked, "What do you write about?" I said, "Possibility thinking. What do you write about?" He answered, "Applied mathematics." I hoped he wouldn't pursue the conversation. Then I had a revelation: "You know, I write about impossibility and possibility thinkers. Obviously possibility thinking doesn't apply in mathematics. I mean, two plus two equals four, and four plus four equals eight."

And he said, "Doctor Schuller, let me tell you a true story: I was a graduate at Berkeley thirty years ago. I came to class late and copied what I believed to be the homework: two problems that were written on the blackboard. Later I said to my professor, 'I haven't been able to solve the homework problems yet, can I have a little more time?' He said, 'Sure, George. When you do, put it on my desk.'

"In due time I did solve them and turned the homework in. Several weeks later, one Sunday morning, there was a great pounding at my door; it was my professor. He was all excited, for it turned out what I mistook for homework were two famous unsolved problems of mathematical statistics.

"Now, Dr. Schuller, do you suppose I would have solved these two problems if I knew that they were two well-known unsolved problems?"

What keeps the average person from mining his mind and discovering this power God put in it? I can tell you, it is preconceived, prejudicial, negative information that's put into us. We think it's impossible. The most dangerous person on planet earth is the negative-thinking expert. Because he's an expert in his field, nobody challenges him. Therefore you accept it as fact. You spend your life believing the lowest, instead of beginning to believe the possible.

Test Your Possibility
Thinking

Let me ask you a question: Are you a possibility thinker or an impossibility thinker? Here's a test: Tonight the sun will set at approximately 7:30. Suppose it's a beautiful sunset—red, green, purple, blue, orange, and yellow—until twilight and darkness comes and the lights twinkle. Somebody says, "Did you see the sunset?" And you say, "No, I missed it." Is it possible to have a replay? Is it possible to catch the sunset once you've missed it? The answer is no. *Agree?* Wait a minute!

When we left Paris, Mrs. Schuller and I had to get to Honolulu, where I had to deliver the major address to an eight-thousand-member convention. People told me it was impossible to leave Paris and still get to Honolulu on time. There just aren't planes to get you there that fast. Suddenly somebody said, "You can make it if you fly the *Concorde*." So, Mrs. Schuller and I booked ourselves on the *Concorde*. It was 8:00 P.M. when we were to take off. I was excited because the sun was setting at 9:05 P.M., and I expected it would be glorious to catch the sunset at sixty thousand feet in the air. I was told you could see the curvature of the earth at that altitude.

During the takeoff I made this exciting discovery: I can understand Greek, Hebrew, English, and Dutch, but I didn't know I could understand French. As we were powering down the runway, suddenly there was a screech of brakes, smell of rubber, and a Frenchman rattled something off that I understood. He said, *"Le problem,"* and I knew we had a problem.

We went back to the gate and we waited. The sun was dropping lower and lower. Finally at 8:45 the sun was horizontal in its beams. We waited until 10:00 P.M. By now it was very dark. We went back with the lights on in the plane, we took off down the runway, and suddenly we were up in the air. It was an exciting, steep, vertical ascent, like a missile. The flight attendant told us that the screen in the front of the fuselage was not a television screen, but we would see a digital dial and the numbers would register our speed. Suddenly, it was 45, 50, 90, 98, 100—meaning Mach 1—then 1, 2, 3, 4, 5, 6, 7 . . . 198, 199, Mach 2. We were now going over 1,400 miles per hour. Then, out of the blackened window, I could see from the west the horizon. Where moments before it was black, it had now turned gold, then orange, and then streaks of pink, purple, red, and blue. And then it happened—sunrise in the west! The sun began to climb. We literally were catching up with the sunset that we had missed! The whole sun was up in the sky sending its late afternoon sunlight into the fuselage. The flight attendant came to me and said, "Doctor Schuller, the pilot would like to invite you to the cockpit." As I went into the cockpit, we were going Mach 2.4. And the cockpit was bathed in golden sunlight.

Today I can tell you it's possible to have a replay of the sunset if you've missed it, given the right circumstances and conditions. A year ago, I would have told you it's impossible. What is my point? My point is: What may be impossible today, may be possible tomorrow.

R. G. LeTourneau

Robert G. LeTourneau was probably one of the great geniuses of our time and a great Christian. He had the subcontractor's job for the Hoover Dam. He had underestimated, because he ran into deep, solid rock and the cost for fulfilling his commitment bankrupted him. In deep despair he turned to God and became a believer. Napoleon Hill traveled with him for one and a half years and tells this story: "One night when LeTourneau finished his lecture, he and I went into his private plane. The pilot took off, and LeTourneau sat on one side and I sat on the other. It wasn't long before LeTourneau was praying silently, and in his prayers he fell asleep. He was a huge bulk of a man and he was sleeping deeply." Napoleon Hill said, "I've seen people walk in their sleep before, but I've never seen anything like this.

"In his sleep, LeTourneau reached in his pocket, pulled out a notebook and a pencil, wrote something in the notebook, and put it back in his pocket without opening his eyes. When we landed and he awoke, I said, 'Mr. LeTourneau, do you remember writing in the notebook?' He said no. He quickly reached into his pocket, pulled out his notebook, and was shocked to see what he had written. He said, 'That's the answer I've been searching for! That's the solution to the problem! The invention is now complete!' " And he built his huge earth-moving equipment, and that's how the breakthrough came to him.

Mine your mind. Get in touch with God. He made your mind and He can tell you how to mine it! When He does, look out!

Mom's Hot Apple Pie

My mother was a remarkable woman, and the most powerful encourager in my lifetime. She was also my favorite cook and my chief critic. She was married for fifty-three years to my father, a simple Iowa farmer. And many times she probably felt she led an obscure and unimportant life. Often she failed to see the significance of her human existence. The most important accomplishments of her life were to raise her five children, take care of her husband, and find pride in one special talent—baking apple pies. (That talent plagued me with a weight problem for many years, and I no longer eat apple pies!)

Twelve years ago, I received a phone call. "Bob," said the strained voice on the other end of the line, "your mother is very sick." I immediately boarded the first available plane and flew to northwest Iowa. But before the plane touched down in Sioux Falls, my mother had already passed away. I talked to the pastor who was with her shortly before she died. He shared with me her final request: "Read Isaiah forty-three, verses one through four," she said, "Fear not. . . ." "Yes," her pastor replied, "I know the passage: Fear not. For when you go through the waters, they will not overflow you. When you go through the fire, it will not consume you. For I am your God. I have redeemed you. I know your name; you are mine. I will be with you." And she was comforted.

Recently I received a simple little letter postmarked IOWA, and inside was a check for $68,400.00—the second-largest unsolicited check we'd ever received. I called the lady to make sure that we should accept this donation, because the shaky handwriting was obviously that of an older woman. We didn't want to leave someone destitute. When I got her on the phone, it quickly became apparent that she possessed a keen mind. We had a very exciting conversation. "You know," I said, "I'm from Iowa. I grew up in a little town you probably never heard of; it's called 'Alton.' " "I know," she replied, "I was born in Alton." "You were born in Alton?" I asked in astonishment. "Yes," she said. "As a young girl, I left to become a schoolteacher. When I started teaching, I began a little savings account and put some of each week's salary into that savings. Now I'm getting on in years and I'm alone; I never married. I've got a wonderful, tiny little house—I call it my dream house. It doesn't cost anything to keep it up.

"And you know," she continued, "I suddenly thought about the savings account. I hadn't looked at it for years. When I checked up on it, I discovered it had grown these many years to $68,400.00—just out of a schoolteacher's salary. Isn't that incredible?" "It sure is!" I exclaimed. "Since I don't have a family or anyone close," she explained, "I've decided I want to give this money to the Crystal Cathedral."

"You say you were born in Alton," I interjected. "Did you ever know, by any chance, my mother, Jenny Beltman Schuller?" "Oh, I sure did," she replied. "I'll never forget her. In fact, I'm so grateful to her. One time my sister got sick, and your mother came over and gave her an apple pie."

When God delivers us from evil, He turns us into

beautiful people. He gives us a calling; maybe it's making apple pies or giving gifts of money, love, or services. But remember, any fool can count the seeds in an apple, but only God can count the apples in a seed. If you ask God to save you, He'll save you for eternity. And He'll use you in ways you won't even know about. Believe me, God will do something wonderful with the life you give to Him!

A Boost From Pope John Paul II

When I was in Rome, one of my most wonderful experiences was watching Pope John Paul II receive his audiences. Thirty thousand people from all over the world—Japan, South America, England, Ireland, Italy, America, and Poland were assembled in Saint Peter's Square. A fence separated the masses from the pope as he sat on his throne with secretaries on either side. To his right were the cardinals, some visiting bishops and a few chairs for a small number of honored persons, among whom I was included.

Since I was sitting in the front row about fourteen feet from the Holy Father, I was able to observe his face and eyes very clearly as he received his audiences.

Finally the group from Poland was recognized. The pope looked at them and smiled as he read something to them in Polish. The secretary was about to announce another group, thus signifying the end of the audience. But the Polish group was not about to be cut off. Without invitation or approval, they began to sing a song—their national anthem.

For the first time during the entire one and a half hours the pope was receiving people, he dropped his head—I suspect, to hide his tears. What must he have been thinking? Was he remembering his ties to Poland, his homeland? Or was he reminding himself of his new loyalties to his own state, the Vatican? Whatever he was thinking, it was clear that he was deeply moved. For halfway through the anthem he raised his head and sang the rest of the song with his countrymen. I must admit, a tear or two rolled out of my eyes. He showed his loyalty to his roots. He gave his own people the boost they needed.

The Parthenon

I remember the first time I saw the Parthenon in Athens. I've always considered it once of the most beautiful works of architecture in the world. When I stood looking at the smooth, white marble columns, however, I had the most sickening feeling. There, in one of the columns, was a rusty old bridge spike, about eight inches long, wedged into a crack. It was ghastly. "Who did that?" I asked my guide, as I pointed to the spike. "Some vandal?" "Oh, no," replied, "that was driven in there when the barbarians took over. They hammered nails into the columns and hung ropes between them. That's where they dried their laundry."

A truly beautiful person helps us become sensitive to the wonders around us. He helps us appreciate our own potential and encourages us to become all that we can be. He enables us to worship God in the beauty of holiness by helping us to become whole and complete ourselves.

Give It All You've Got

Not long ago I checked into a hotel back East. It was late in the evening, and the lobby was empty except for the desk clerk. I checked in and began to unpack quickly, so I could get some rest. As I reached for my toothbrush, I realized that I had forgotten to pack my toothpaste. "Well, no problem," I thought to myself. "There's a dispenser down the hall." So I walked down the hall and stood before the machine studying the contents. Enclosed behind the glass were all kinds of goodies—razor blades, pocketbooks, combs, and little tubes of toothpaste! All I had to do was insert two quarters into the slot and my problem would be solved. I had no change, so I went to the desk and got four quarters. When I returned to the dispenser I dropped in the first quarter . . . *cling.* Then I inserted the second quarter . . . *cling.* I pushed the red button below the tube of toothpaste and waited. Nothing happened! It didn't work! So I pressed the coin lever, and my quarters returned.

Okay, I thought, *let's give it another try.* I dropped the first quarter in . . . *cling.* Then the second quarter . . . *cling.* (I even used the other two quarters for good luck!) I pushed the button—again nothing happened! Still no toothpaste! I paused for a moment staring at all the things behind that glass—just out of my reach. "Think positive," I said aloud. So I pressed the button again. Nothing!

A little frustrated at this point, I pushed the coin-return lever, recovered my quarters and stood in front of that stubborn machine. It had what I needed but it wouldn't release what it had to offer! I was willing to cooperate. I had a positive attitude toward it. I was willing to pay the price, but it just would not release the valuable contents it held within.

Some of you are like that dispensing machine. Deep within yourself, you have a lot to give, but you don't know how to give it. You have a lot to offer, but something keeps you tied up—feeling timid, shy, retiring, bashful, and inferior. I challenge you to begin to believe that you have something beautiful and positive to give—it's stored up inside of you.

You're Never Too Old

One day I read about a remarkable woman named Eula Weaver. Her picture was in the newspaper and she was in her jogging suit! Now that's not so unusual, except that this woman is eighty-eight years old. Now, what would happen if you were seventy-seven years old and were paralyzed? What thoughts would be going through your head? Perhaps: *Well, this is it, I'm at the age when people die.* Or, *It must be God's will for me to pack up. I'm only three years short of eighty. This is it!*

Not Eula Weaver! She had a stroke at seventy-seven years of age and was paralyzed, but she didn't give up. "I could hardly walk at all," she said. "Doctors gave me two choices. One, to spend the rest of my life as an invalid; or two, get out of bed and start walking—no matter how much it hurt!" That's when she decided to get out and start walking. And today, eleven years later, and two years short of ninety, she's running a mile every day.

Montezuma's Treasure

Down in old Mexico, they jailed a peasant who had lived in a tar-paper shack but had recently built a cinderblock house on the beach for his wife and children. Everyone wondered where he got the money. They checked it out and found that he had sold two gold bars to a jeweler. The jeweler had paid him fifty-eight hundred dollars for these two twenty-four-carat gold bars. They had an actual market value of over one-half million dollars! More of the story began to unfold as they checked out the gold bars, until finally the chief archeologists in Mexico affirmed that these two gold bars are part of Montezuma's lost treasure. Now some of you may know that the greatest lost, undiscovered treasure today on planet earth is Montezuma's gold. At the end of the sixteenth century, this Aztec ruler (who had acquired the greatest amassed fortune in gold bars in any civilization) saw his fall coming—and indeed, his empire was abolished by Cortez. Now what we don't know is what happened to Montezuma's gold. But suddenly a peasant had found a few of the gold bars. Does this mean now that we're close to discovering the whole treasure?

I'm not suggesting you go look for Montezuma's treasure. What I am suggesting is this: The greatest discovery yet to be made is the discovery of the opportunities that you have in living—the undeveloped, nonactualized potential within you that waits to be discovered like a lost treasure.

The Devil's Plan

I will not quit! I say to you that these four words are God's antidote to man's biggest emotional problem. And what is that? Man's biggest emotional problem is *discouragement.*

A purely mythological and legendary story has been created to prove this point. It was fabricated to tell a very authentic illustration. When Satan got all his cohorts together and saw that the Christians were doing a lot of good in this world, and that Jesus did make a lot of difference, he said, "Look, we've got a problem. Jesus Christ has created a big problem for us. What are we going to do?" One of the devil's cohorts said, "I've got a good idea. We'll get into the brains of all the Christian men and women and we'll fill them with lust. That will really knock them out." They had a big discussion, but they couldn't make a decision. Another devil said, "No, that isn't going to work because these Christians love each other. And people who really know how to love never give in to lust. People who are used to quality are never going to buy something that cheap. That won't work."

Then another devil came up with this idea: "Let's get all these Christians so filled with selfishness that we'll tell them to love money, and they'll be so hung up on money that they'll go to hell." They talked about it and decided it was a great idea to appeal to the materialistic instincts. They thought about it a little more and Satan said, "I don't think it will work. These Christians will just go out and make all the money they can, and then they'll give away all they can. That's what's going to happen. If you get them thinking about money, they won't be against it. They'll be for it. They'll make a lot and give it away, and the movement will spread because they feed it. That's a lousy idea."

Finally one little devil came up with the best idea. "Let's fill them with discouragement! If we get them discouraged, we'll just get them thinking and looking at all the rest of the deviltry and sin going on in the world. They'll look at all the people who don't follow Jesus. We'll get them discouraged. If we get them discouraged, we've got it made. Because if we get them discouraged, they'll become cynical. When they become cynical, they won't believe in hope anymore. And when they don't believe in hope, they will be despairing. And once they're despairing, they'll be defeated." And all the chorus of devils applauded and said, "That's the key. *Discouragement* is of the devil!"

I WILL NOT QUIT! is in the heart of every winner. And if you could look into the heart of a defeated person, you will find the words *I quit*. Great people are common people committed to uncommon goals.

You're Twice My Boat

Once there was a little boy who made a sailboat. He carefully carved it; sanded it; painted it; and made a beautiful sail. When he finished it, he couldn't wait to see if it would sail, so he took it down to the lake. He found a nice grassy spot by the edge of the water, got down on all fours and gently set the boat in the water. Then he blew a little puff of air and waited. The boat didn't move. So he blew a little harder, until the wind caught the sail and the boat started moving. "It sails! It sails!" he cried out, clapping his hands and dancing along the side of the lake. But then he stopped. He realized that he had forgotten to tie a string onto the end of the boat. He watched it going farther and farther away, until it was out of his reach.

The little boy was both happy and sad. He was thrilled that it sailed, but saddened because it was now out of his reach. He ran home crying.

Sometime later he was wandering through town, when he passed a toy store that sold both new and old toys. And there in the window was his boat! He was ecstatic! He ran in and said, "That's my boat! That's my boat!" The shop owner looked down at the little boy and said, "I'm sorry, I bought the boat. It is for sale, though." "But it's my boat," the boy cried out. "I made it, I sailed it. I lost it! It's mine!" "I'm sorry," the shop owner exclaimed, "I bought it. If you want to buy it, you may have it." "How much is it?" the lad asked. And when he found out how much it was, he went home very sad.

But this little boy was very determined. When he got home he went to his room and counted his pennies, nickels, dimes, and quarters. He still needed a little more money before he could buy back his precious boat. So he worked and saved, until finally he had just the right amount. He ran back to the store, hoping the boat would still be there. There it was sitting in the window, just as before.

He ran into the shop, dug into his pockets, and placed all of his money onto the counter. "I want to buy my boat," he enthused. The shopkeeper lifted the little sailboat out of the window and placed it into the excited boy's hands. He grasped the boat, holding it tightly to his chest, and ran home proudly, saying, "You are my boat. You are my boat! You're twice my boat. First, you are my boat because I made you; and second, you are my boat because I bought you!"

If you were the boat, you would know that you were loved. It's a choice, not a chance. The news I have, my friend, is this: You are that sailboat! Jesus Christ is the little boy. And the cross is the price! You are God's child twice over. First you were God's child because He made you; and second, you are God's child because He bought you on the cross of Calvary!

Prosperity Through Possibility Thinking

As I've mentioned before, these days I'm raising fish. Actually I have been for some years. I raise Japanese carp known as koi fish. Several years ago I bought a bunch of little teeny ones for three dollars apiece.

Since then, they've grown and reproduced. Today I have a few hundred of these beautiful Japanese koi fish. They're friends of mine, each with a distinct personality. Some are nice; some aren't so nice. In a way, my fish remind me of people.

If I sit at the edge of the pond and watch a leaf fall into the water, I notice that most of the fish will scatter and flee in all directions, as the leaf hits the surface. But there are a few—only a few—who will not flee to hiding places when something hits the water's surface. They are the big fish who make a slow curve around the new object, inspecting it carefully and cautiously. They know that what they find might not be an enemy, but might, in fact, be food.

These are the fish who always find the food. That's why they're the big fish. Frightened fish stay skinny. And a frightened society will soon become an impoverished society. Productivity will stop, and the inevitable conditions of recession and inflation will degenerate into economic depression. There is nothing we need more in the United States today than *possibility thinking*. Possibility thinking works wonders because people dare to take some risks on the odds that if they make it, they can do a lot of good for a lot of people.

"We Call Him Schuller"

We live on a few acres in what was "the country" when we bought it several years ago. During the time I've spent in our home there, I've enjoyed many hobbies. I have several ponds on my property and so, at one point I decided to buy some ducks. Unfortunately the ducks flew south for the winter and never returned. Then I bought three beautiful snow-white geese. They were gorgeous creatures, but also messy and disagreeable in temperament. Two of them came to an untimely end when they decided to tangle with the dogs and lost. That left one beautiful white goose. About a year ago, I decided to give him to an electrician who did some work on our house. He took the goose to his ranch home. Just the other day the man came back to visit and showed me a picture of the goose. "Boy is he big!" I exclaimed when he showed me the picture. "He sure is," the man replied. "He dominates the farm. He runs all over the place, flapping his wings, and honking incessantly. We call him 'Schuller.'"

Make the Ending Glorious

When I was a little boy, I studied piano, and my mother was my teacher. When it came time for a recital, my mother made me go over the conclusion again and again. I had to get it down perfect! "Keep on practicing the conclusion, Bob. Learn those last measures!" she used to say. "Look, Bob, you can make a mistake in the beginning; or you can make a mistake in the middle; the people will forget it—if you make the ending glorious!"

Make the ending glorious! I don't know what kind of childhood you had. I don't know what kind of life you had. I don't know where you are now! But where you are now, Jesus is present. Take Him into your life now, and I can tell you the ending will be *glorious!*

Index of Names

Index of Titles

Index of Topics

A Lifetime of Answers...

JOVE INSPIRATION BOOKS